HARD TIMES BY CHARLES DICKENS

£1-00

MACMILLAN MASTER GUIDES

General Editor: James Gibson

Also published by Macmillan

MACMILLAN MASTER SERIES

Mastering English Literature R. Gill
Mastering English Language S. H. Burton
Mastering English Grammar S. H. Burton

MACMILLAN MASTER GUIDES

HARD TIMES

BY CHARLES DICKENS

NORMAN PAGE

MACMILLAN

First edition 1985

Published by
MACMILLAN EDUCATION LTD
Houndmills, Basingstoke, Hampshire RG21 2XS
and London
Companies and representatives
throughout the world

Printed in Hong Kong
ISBN 0-333-39002-4 Pbk
ISBN 0-333-39902-1 Pbk export

CONTENTS

vi

GENERAL EDITOR'S PREFACE

The aim of the Macmillan Master Guides is to help you to appreciate the book you are studying by providing information about it and by suggesting ways of reading and thinking about it which will lead to a fuller understanding. The section on the writer's life and background has been designed to illustrate those aspects of the writer's life which have influenced the work, and to place it in its personal and literary context. The summaries and critical commentary are of special importance in that each brief summary of the action is followed by an examination of the significant critical points. The space which might have been given to repetitive explanatory notes has been devoted to a detailed analysis of the kind of passage which might confront you in an examination. Literary criticism is concerned with both the broader aspects of the work being studied and with its detail. The ideas which meet us in reading a great work of literature, and their relevance to us today, are an essential part of our study, and our Guides look at the thought of their subject in some detail. But just as essential is the craft with which the writer has constructed his work of art, and this is considered under several technical headings - characterisation, language, style and stagecraft.

The authors of these Guides are all teachers and writers of wide experience, and they have chosen to write about books they admire and know well in the belief that they can communicate their admiration to you. But you yourself must read and know intimately the book you are studying. No one can do that for you. You should see this book as a lamppost. Use it to shed light, not to lean against. If you know your text and know what it is saying about life, and how it says it, then you will enjoy it, and there is no better way of passing an examination in literature.

JAMES GIBSON

ACKNOWLEDGEMENT

Cover Illustration: *Awaiting Admission to the Casual Ward* by Sir Luke Fildes. © Royal Holloway College, University of London, courtesy of the Bridgeman Art Library.

1 LIFE AND BACKGROUND

Charles Dickens was born on 7 February 1812 in Portsmouth, where his father was a clerk in the Navy Pay Office. George III was still king, but from 1811 his son (later George IV) acted as Prince Regent on account of his father's incapacity. We naturally think of Dickens as a Victorian, but it is important to remember that his childhood and early youth were spent in the pre-Victorian period, when manners and morals were very different from those customarily associated with the term 'Victorian', and that he was twenty-five when the Queen came to the throne. Dickens was born into a world without railways or the penny post; his lifetime was to witness more dramatic changes in society and human life than had ever taken place in the history of the world, and many of these changes are vividly recorded in the novels he published between 1836 and 1870.

His father's job as a minor civil servant involved the family in fairly frequent moves, and before Dickens was three they were installed in London, where he was to spend most of his life, though from 1817 to 1822 they lived at Chatham in Kent. John Dickens's income, though not large, ought to have been sufficient to keep them in reasonable middle-class comfort, and at various times they lived in pleasant houses and employed one or two servants. But John Dickens, who was later to be good-humouredly portrayed as Mr Micawber in *David Copperfield*, habitually lived beyond his means; and matters came to a head early in 1824, when he was arrested for debt and sent to the Marshalsea Prison. A week or two earlier young Charles, now almost twelve years old, had been sent out to work in a rat-infested warehouse by the Thames. There he pasted labels on pots of boot-blacking and suffered a depression of spirits that haunted him for the rest of his life; indeed, it has been suggested that his lifelong concern for the outcast and the underdog, and especially for unfortunate and unhappy children, stems from this bitter experience.

The experience lasted only a few months, but of course the young Dickens had no means of knowing at the time that it would not last for ever. As it turned out, his father obtained his release and Charles was taken away from the factory and sent to a private school, Wellington House Academy, where he spent about three years. At fifteen he left school and obtained a job as office-boy for a solicitor; but this was not likely to satisfy his energy or his ambitions for long, and in his spare time he studied shorthand. As a result, before he was seventeen, he had become a free-lance shorthand-reporter in the courts – the first step on the road to becoming a journalist and, eventually, a professional author. During this period of his life he spent a good deal of time at the theatre, and even thought seriously of becoming a professional actor. The passion for the stage remained with him for life, and has left its unmistakable mark on his writings – in, for example, his habit of conceiving and presenting action in theatrical terms. (Consider in *Hard Times*, among many other instances, the two big scenes between Louisa and her father, the scene between Sissy and Harthouse, and the death of Stephen Blackpool.)

By 1832, when he was twenty, Dickens had established himself as a reporter and was rapidly acquiring a reputation for speed and accuracy. It was a period of intense political activity, stimulated by the passage of the 1832 Reform Bill, and during the next two or three years he travelled widely to cover elections, political meetings and speeches by important politicians. Meanwhile he had begun to write short fictional sketches that dealt realistically with aspects of London life, especially the life of the poorer classes. The first of these was published at the end of 1833; and many others followed, later collected as *Sketches by Boz*, a volume published on his twenty-fourth birthday.

The year 1836 was a turning-point in Dickens's life. Early in the year he was invited to write the text to accompany a series of illustrations by a well-known artist, and in this unlikely way was born his first novel, *The Pickwick Papers*. With a force of character that was never to diminish, Dickens took over the enterprise and adapted it to his own purposes, so that the original idea was abandoned and the result was a long novel with illustrations. It was published in instalments, the first appearing on 31 March; two days later Dickens married Catherine Hogarth, the daughter of a fellow-journalist.

Within a few months *Pickwick* became the rage: all England was talking about it, and Dickens found himself suddenly famous. In the ensuing years he produced a stream of novels, not merely in rapid succession but sometimes simultaneously, and his fame spread throughout the world. In 1842, for instance, he made a triumphant tour of America, where he was given royal treatment. His seemingly boundless energies led him to throw himself into innumerable undertakings and relationships. For twenty years he edited and closely supervised the contents of a weekly magazine – a task that many might have considered a full-time employment, but which for Dickens was merely one among many other activities. He was much in demand as a public speaker and had the reputation of being one of the best after-dinner speakers in England. From 1858 he gave public readings of his work for profit (he had done so earlier for charity), and eventually gave over five hundred of these one-man shows in Britain and America with extraordinary success. He had a wide circle of friends, and threw himself into an active social life. He travelled widely, and spent long periods residing on the Continent. He loved to organise amateur theatricals, and toured England with his company of players (himself being, needless to say, producer and star of the show), performing even before the Queen herself. And he enjoyed family life with his nine surviving children, though in later years his marriage deteriorated and he and his wife were legally separated in 1858.

Added to all this, and more important than anything else, he produced a series of masterpieces that led to his recognition as the greatest Victorian novelist and one of the greatest figures in English literature. He was still hard at work, half-way through his last novel, *The Mystery of Edwin Drood*, when he died suddenly in 1870.

Dickens was a great entertainer, but he was also a passionate critic of his times. His journalistic training, combined with his extraordinary powers of observation (his friend the actor William Macready said that he had a 'clutching eye'), enabled him to create in detail a panoramic picture of the age in which he lived: in a brilliant phrase his contemporary Walter Bagehot said that he wrote like 'a special correspondent for posterity'. And much of what he saw and recorded profoundly disturbed his sense of justice and compassion. In his early novels he attacks specific institutions (the Poor Law and the workhouses in *Oliver Twist*, for instance, and the private boarding-schools in *Nicholas Nickleby*); but in his later work he offers a more fundamental, and often more pessimistic, diagnosis of the ills of society.

That much was wrong with society there could be little doubt. England was a land of extremes, of the wealthy living in splendid style and of masses of the poor herded together in urban slums in which hunger, misery and infectious diseases were rampant (this is to say nothing of the misery of those working on the land, of whom Dickens knew little and wrote little). The Industrial Revolution and the population explosion had produced social problems on a colossal scale: not only were they difficult to deal with, however, but many members of the ruling classes denied that they existed. If we think of the Industrial Revolution as beginning about 1780, it was of course well under way by the time Dickens was born, though he managed to catch glimpses of a vanishing world – his grandmother, for instance, was housekeeper in a nobleman's country house. Although Dickens's own family knew poverty and hardship, they never sank to the lowest levels of society; but Dickens had seen the squalor and wretchedness of the urban poor for himself on the long and often solitary walks he took at night through the streets of London, and his interest in social problems and social reform led him to make many visits to prisons, lunatic asylums and other institutions.

Hard Times, coming as it does about half-way through Dickens's career as a novelist, seems to represent a transitional stage between his satire on particular aspects of society and his more general, and gloomier, depiction of its wrongs. The educational methods of the school founded and supervised by Mr Gradgrind are shown to be misguided and harmful in their effects; but the implication is that if different and more enlightened methods were used, all would be well. Such is not the case, however, with the plight of the Coketown operatives: the factory system, whereby thousands toiled for starvation wages so that a few could become rich, is not capable of such ready reform, and Dickens's attitude to it seems at times to be similar to that uttered by Stephen Blackpool in his despair: all a muddle!

Whether a writer can exert an influence on events and, for example, bring about a change in the laws is difficult if not impossible to prove; but there can be little doubt that Dickens modified the climate of opinion, and his ultimate influence, though not quantifiable, may be none the less real. Not only did he enjoy a wide readership, but his readers came from all classes of society. (His official biographer, John Forster, tells a very pleasant story of an elderly charwoman who 'lodged at a snuff-shop' and would gather with her fellow-lodgers once a month to drink tea and listen to their landlord read aloud the latest

instalment of *Dombey and Son*.) One of the ways in which he established a close relationship with his audience – closer than any modern
novelist can hope to achieve – was by the fact that all his novels were
serialised before being published in bound volumes; and since this also
had important effects upon the planning and writing of the novels, it
needs to be briefly described.

Most of Dickens's novels were published in monthly 'numbers'
– paper-covered booklets of thirty-two pages – over a period of about a
year and a half; but a few, including *Hard Times*, appeared in a different
form, being serialised in magazines. This meant, of course, that the
reader did not have the entire book in his hands when he began to read
the novel: indeed, it was not even written. Waiting for the next week's
instalment would increase interest and suspense and would encourage
people to discuss the novel, since they would inevitably all be reading
the same portion at the same time. Moreover, the novelist would receive
'feedback' from sales figures, fan mail and the comments of friends,
so that he might modify certain elements in the story as it went along.
A close parallel is with a television soap opera, to which many of the
same considerations apply.

What effect would this have upon the structure and style of the
novel? Since the weekly portions were quite short (in the case of *Hard
Times* never more than three chapters and usually only one or two),
great concentration of effect was necessary: hence, for instance, the
highly compressed style of the opening passage of the novel, which
begins much more abruptly than most nineteenth-century novels. In
every instalment the threads of what had gone before had to be picked
up; the action had to be significantly advanced; and the next and later
instalments had to be in some slight degree anticipated (or, as Dickens
liked to say, 'foreshadowed'). The novelist also had to help his readers
to remember his characters and the ramifications of his plot from week
to week: after all, even the slowest modern reader is unlikely to spend
nineteen weeks reading *Hard Times*, but the original readers had no
choice (see below for details). As a result Dickens uses a plot that
contains secrets, mysteries, disappearances and reappearances, in an
attempt to sustain interest and give unity to the separate portions of
the novel. His characterisation, too, must be bold and emphatic: there
is little room for subtlety. Dickens helps us to remember his characters
and identify them on their reappearance partly by giving them out-
landish names such as M'Choakumchild and Sparsit, and partly by
giving them highly individual mannerisms of speech such as Sleary's

lisp and Stephen's dialect.

Hard Times was written for Dickens's own weekly magazine, *Household Words*, which had begun publication in 1850.* By the end of 1853, sales were dropping off rather alarmingly; and Dickens decided to come to the rescue by writing a novel, knowing that his great reputation would be likely to boost sales. He began writing early in the new year, and at about the same time he paid a visit to Preston in Lancashire, to observe the strike of millworkers that was in progress there. We must not assume that Coketown is to be precisely identified with Preston – the creative mind does not work in such simple and straightforward ways – but Dickens certainly made use of what he saw there. From an article, 'On Strike', which he published in *Household Words* on 11 February, we know that he attended a meeting of strikers. Since, up to that time, his experience of the industrial north of England had been very limited, he may also have gained valuable information concerning, for instance, the physical appearance of a manufacturing town and the local dialect.

Serialisation began on 1 April and continued for twenty issues until 12 August. Composition of the novel had not been completed until 17 July. Soon after the serial was concluded, the novel was published in volume form, and at this stage Dickens added the titles to the chapters and 'Books' as well as a dedication to that eloquent denouncer of the ills of Victorian society, the historian and social critic Thomas Carlyle. Before he finished, Dickens had found the writing of *Hard Times* a painful business, largely as a result of the shortness of the instalments within which he had to work. As he remarked in a letter to a friend, 'The difficulty of the space is CRUSHING.' In April, when serialisation had begun and when he was therefore under considerable pressure, he wrote to his sub-editor: 'I am in a dreary state, planning and planning the story of Hard times (out of materials for I don't know how long a story) . . . . ' It is interesting to consider what Dickens would have

*In the very first issue of *Household Words* (30 March 1850), Dickens defined his purpose and policy in the magazine as follows:

> No mere utilitarian spirit, no iron binding of the mind to firm realities, will give a harsh tone . . . . we would tenderly cherish the light of Fancy which is inherent in the human breast; which, according to its nurture, burns with an inspiring flame, or sinks into a sullen glare, but which (or woe betide that day!) can never be extinguished.

In a very striking way this anticipates *Hard Times* four years later, especially in its antithesis of 'Fancy' and the 'utilitarian spirit'.

done if he had had more elbow-room (as it is, *Hard Times* is the shortest
of his novels, being only about one-third the length of its immediate
predecessor, *Bleak House*); and it is useful to consider in detail what
artistic results, for better or worse, followed from the 'crushing' limi-
tation upon space. The technique of constructing and composing a
novel for serialisation was a complex and in some ways a very difficult
affair; and even though we no longer read Dickens's novels in the form
in which his first readers encountered them, the effects of serialisation
are still plain to see.

2 SUMMARY AND CRITICAL COMMENTARY

The setting is Coketown, an industrial community in the north of England, and the main plot concerns one of its leading citizens, Mr Thomas Gradgrind, and his family. Gradgrind is a convinced advocate of the utilitarian philosophy of 'fact', and has brought up his children on this principle as well as spreading it more widely through a school that he has established. The story concerns the fates of his two eldest children, Tom and Louisa, and, to a lesser extent, of two of the pupils at the school, Sissy Jupe and Bitzer.

As a result of their imagination and sense of beauty being starved throughout childhood, Tom and Louisa grow up to be bored and discontented, and in different ways their lives come to disaster. Tom robs the bank at which he works and has to flee the country; Louisa makes an unhappy marriage with Josiah Bounderby, a prosperous local business man, and after almost succumbing to the temptation offered by a would-be seducer, the upper-class politician James Harthouse, she leaves her husband and returns home. Bitzer also illustrates the unfortunate influence of the system of education he receives, and proves to be thoroughly selfish and ungrateful; Sissy, on the other hand, has been brought up in a circus and remains untouched by the influence of her schooling, her natural goodness and instinctive wisdom enabling her to help Louisa in her difficulties.

The sub-plot concerns a Coketown mill-worker, Stephen Blackpool, who is unable to obtain a divorce from a drunken wife who causes him much misery and to marry a good woman, Rachael, whom he loves. Stephen is first ostracised by his fellow-workmen because he refuses to join a trade union, then accused of the bank robbery of which Tom is guilty. His name is eventually cleared, but only after he has met his death by falling down a disused mine-shaft.

By the end of the novel, Mr Gradgrind, whose wife has died, whose son is disgraced and exiled, and whose daughter's life is in ruins, has been brought to see the error of his ways and is a much sadder but also a much wiser man.

Each of the thirty-seven chapters of *Hard Times* is examined below from two points of view: (1) the content of the chapter (i.e. a brief summary of the main incidents and conversations that it contains and of its contribution to the development of the action); and (2) matters of interest in relation to interpretation and criticism, the most important of these being discussed more thoroughly in the next two chapters.

As already indicated, *Hard Times* appeared originally as a weekly serial. When Dickens prepared it for volume-publication, he divided it into three sections, to each of which he gave a title: 'Book the First: Sowing' (sixteen chapters), 'Book the Second: Reaping' (twelve chapters), 'Book the Third: Garnering' (nine chapters). Since this division and these subtitles obviously had significance for Dickens, they are preserved in modern editions; and throughout the present book all references are given to both 'Book' and chapter. Thus, I,2 means the second chapter of the first book.

Summary

I, 1. This very short chapter sets the opening scene, 'a plain, bare, monotonous vault of a schoolroom', and introduces a speaker as yet unnamed. In a 'dictatorial' voice he is insisting that all that is needed in education and in life is facts.

Commentary

By using the classroom setting, Dickens immediately launches into one of the main themes of his novel: what kind of education is best? 'Facts', which appears in the opening sentence, will turn out to be one of the key-words of the novel; and the speaker's statement in the opening paragraph that 'This is the principle on which I bring up my own children' makes the reader wonder how this system will work out and thus points forward to one of the major areas of plot-interest, the fate of Louisa and Tom. In all these ways, Dickens gets his novel off to a very brisk start – perhaps because he is mindful of the strictly limited space available in a weekly serial. Note, too, the stylised and symbolical elements in the description of the speaker, whose 'square forefinger' and 'square coat, square legs, square shoulders' suggest the rigid and mechanical nature of his educational philosophy.

Summary

I,2. The speaker is now identified as Mr Thomas Gradgrind. He questions two of the pupils: Sissy (short for Cecilia) Jupe, whose father works with horses in a circus, is unable to provide a definition of a horse when it is asked for; but Bitzer, who is clearly a model pupil, obliges with a prompt definition crammed with 'facts'. The class is also questioned by a government official concerned with education. The third adult present, the schoolmaster Mr M'Choakumchild, is also introduced and the training he has received is ironically described.

Commentary

The title, 'Murdering the Innocents', alludes to Herod's slaughter of the male infants (see Matthew ii). Proper names such as Gradgrind and M'Choakumchild have an obviously suggestive and symbolic purpose (for further discussion of this point, see p. 59 below). The questioning of the children embodies Dickens's satire on the Victorian enthusiasm for 'useful knowledge', and the introduction in the last sentence of the chapter of the word 'Fancy' provides an antithesis to 'Facts' that will recur throughout the novel. This antithesis is dramatised in the characters of the two pupils, Sissy and Bitzer. Whereas Sissy (referred to by Mr Gradgrind as 'Girl number twenty', a precise but dehumanising label) is 'dark-eyed and dark-haired' and seems to have her natural colouring enriched by the sunbeam that strikes her, Bitzer is 'light-eyed and light-haired' and seems drained and almost rendered bloodless by the sunlight. His eyes are described as 'cold', and the contrast between his coldness and Sissy's warmth is developed later. Note the irony and absurdity of the system that brands Sissy, who has grown up among horses, a failure for not being ready with an arid verbal definition of a horse, whereas Bitzer, whose knowledge is *merely* verbal and not backed by any felt experience, comes off best.

Summary

I,3. The chapter opens with an account of the upbringing that has been bestowed on Mr Gradgrind's five children and a description of his house, the aptly-named Stone Lodge. As he walks home from the school, Gradgrind passes the circus at which Sissy's father is employed and is amazed to see two of his children, Louisa (aged fifteen or sixteen) and Tom, trying to catch a glimpse of the circus through a gap in the fence. When Louisa is asked by her father why she is doing such a thing, she tells him that she has been 'tired a long time . . . of everything'. The chapter ends with a reference to a character not yet introduced: 'What would Mr Bounderby say?'

Commentary

Mr Gradgrind has been consistent in subjecting his own children to the same system of education as is implemented at his school. They have never been allowed to hear nursery rhymes or fairy stories, which represent 'fancy' or nourishment for the imagination, but have been given a diet of hard facts. But this has had the effect of leaving the older children unsatisfied and discontented – hence Louisa's admission of her boredom, the surreptitious peeping at the circus, and much else that follows. Dickens's pattern of contrasts between the circus and all that Gradgrind stands for is now beginning to emerge. As for the Gradgrind home, it symbolises the Gradgrind philosophy: its strict symmetry is like a calculation in arithmetic, and even the lawn and garden, where some signs of natural growth might be expected, are 'ruled straight like a botanical account-book'. The chapter-title, 'A Loophole', is deliberately ambiguous, not only referring to the gap in the fence through which Louisa and Tom glimpse a world of magic that has been denied to them, but also hinting at something missing in the upbringing they have received. The reference to Mr Bounderby at the end of the chapter arouses a curiosity on the reader's part that is satisfied in the next chapter (though the original readers had to wait a whole week before the new instalment, beginning at Chapter 4, came into their hands).

Summary

I,4. Mr Josiah Bounderby is introduced and identified as 'a rich man: banker, merchant, manufacturer, and what not'. He is a boastful, overbearing, self-made man who frequently refers to his humble origins and early disadvantages in a manner that makes them a source of pride. (He claims to have been ill treated and cast upon the world at a young age, and to have made his way by his own unaided efforts.) Mrs Gradgrind, a timid and feeble woman, crushed by the strength of her husband's convictions, is also introduced. Gradgrind and Bounderby discuss Louisa and Tom's behaviour, and Bounderby attributes it to 'idle imagination' and persuades Gradgrind to turn Sissy out of the school as a bad influence. When Bounderby leaves, he kisses Louisa, who after his departure rubs the cheek he has kissed 'until it was burning red'.

Commentary

Although there are some superficial similarities between Gradgrind and Bounderby – the former is an M.P., the latter a successful man of business, hence both are powerful in their influence upon society, and both are self-confident and emphatic in manner – the difference between them is already apparent. Gradgrind's convictions, though sadly misguided, are perfectly sincere: he honestly believes that his doctrines are for the good of society and the individuals that compose it. Bounderby, on the other hand, is egocentric, indifferent to the feelings of others and, for all his harping on his humble origins, a proud and self-important man. The relationship of Bounderby and Louisa to be presented later in the novel is already foreshadowed in this early chapter, and even its outcome is hinted at in Louisa's passionate gesture.

Summary

I,5. Coketown, the northern industrial town that is the setting of the novel, is described. On their way to see Sissy's father in order to tell him that Sissy must leave the school, Gradgrind and Bounderby meet Sissy and Bitzer.

Commentary

Dickens's description of Coketown brings together and stresses some of the points made in earlier chapters. It is a town wholly given up to the factory system – that is, to the making of money for the masters and the exploitation of the workers. This 'town of machinery' is mechanical in the monotony of its layout and architecture: the streets and houses have no individuality but seem to repeat each other endlessly, and even the people seem like parts of a machine in their regular movements and repeated operations (compare the attempt in the school to turn the individual children into parts of a smoothly-functioning machine: 'Girl number twenty'). Thus not only the different buildings with different functions (church, jail, hospital, school) are rendered indistinguishable, but the inhabitants are denied their uniqueness as human souls and turned into units in a system that allows them no freedom or spontaneity of behaviour, but imposes on them a strict pattern of monotonously repeated actions. As Dickens sums up: 'Fact, fact, fact, everywhere in the material aspect of the town; fact, fact, fact, everywhere in the immaterial.'

Summary

I,6. Sissy discovers that her father has deserted her. While she searches for him, Gradgrind and Bounderby have a conversation with two circus employees, Kidderminster and Childers. Other circus folk, and Mr Sleary, proprietor of the circus, are also introduced. In view of Sissy's misfortune and her great distress, Gradgrind offers to receive her into his home and to give her an education, on condition that she holds no more communication with the circus folk. She agrees to do so and bids a tearful farewell to her old life.

Commentary

Sissy's introduction into the Gradgrind household will allow Dickens to exploit more fully and dramatically the contrast between her and Louisa and the two educational philosophies they represent. The reader's curiosity is stimulated: will Sissy be changed by her new environment, or will her early upbringing retain its strength and perhaps even bring about change in the Gradgrind family? An interesting technical feature in this chapter is Dickens's fondness for individualising and rendering memorable even his minor characters through their speech (for example, Sleary's lisping dialogue, perhaps an attempt to suggest the slurred speech of a confirmed drinker). Extensive use is also made of circus slang (see p. 63, below), which has the effect of presenting the circus as a colourful and intimate world of its own. Throughout this scene, the contrast of speech, behaviour, outlook and values in the two groups – on the one hand, Gradgrind and Bounderby (i.e. Coketown), on the other hand, the circus (which is only temporarily in Coketown and will soon move on) – is stressed.

Summary

I,7. The scene now moves to Bounderby's house, and his housekeeper, Mrs Sparsit, is introduced. She is an elderly and 'highly connected' widow. Bounderby informs her that he intends to employ Tom Gradgrind in his bank when the boy leaves school. Gradgrind, Louisa and Sissy arrive, and Sissy is told that she will be employed in the Gradgrind household to attend on Mrs Gradgrind, who is 'rather an invalid'. Sissy mentions that she used to read to her father; and when asked what she read, she replies: ' "About the Fairies, sir, and the Dwarf, and the Hunchback, and the Genies" ' – a species of literature that Gradgrind dismisses as 'destructive nonsense'.

Commentary

In this chapter Dickens lays the ground for several later developments. Mrs Sparsit is to be important as a spy and plotter. Her apparent humility and stressing of her role as a servant does not conceal an absurd pride in her aristocratic connections and former social status; although, therefore, she is in some respect the opposite of her employer (he has come up in the world, she has gone down), she resembles him in the importance she attaches to external attributes rather than real worth. For his part, Bounderby, who constantly refers to Mrs Sparsit's former glory, uses her to draw attention to his own status and power – derived, of course, not from birth but from wealth acquired through business ventures. Tom's later employment in the bank, and the disaster it leads to, are also initiated here. Sissy's reference to the books she has read reminds us of her role as the representative of 'fancy' and again makes us wonder what effect she will have upon the Gradgrind household, from which that quality has been sternly banned.

Summary

I,8. Dickens opens this chapter by striking the 'key-note' again (the reference is back to the opening paragraph of Chapter 5). Louisa has been told, as a child, 'never wonder'; and wonder is a quality that has been banished from the lives of the inhabitants of Coketown – not altogether successfully, however, for the factory-workers evince a taste for fiction that is to Mr Gradgrind quite inexplicable. Tom tells Louisa that he is 'tired of my life' and will be glad to leave home when he enters Bounderby's employment. He also makes it clear that he will use Bounderby's evident feelings for Louisa to his own advantage.

Commentary

Like the earlier incident in Chapter 3, when Gradgrind found Tom and Louisa anxious to satisfy their curiosity with a glimpse of the circus, this chapter shows that the Gradgrind system of education has been a failure in human terms, having produced in Tom and Louisa a sense of weariness and discontent, as if they were conscious of something having been missed in life. Again, important later developments are hinted at: Tom's selfish determination to make use of his sister, regardless of her own feelings or interest, hints at the unhappiness that awaits them both.

Summary

I,9. Sissy tells Louisa of her failures at school. She also talks to her about her father, whose sudden departure remains a mystery, but who she is still hoping will return. Tom demands that, when Bounderby visits the house, his sister should put in an appearance even against her own inclinations, since this may lead to some advantage for himself.

Commentary

As in the previous chapter, Tom's heartless selfishness is stressed, he is quite prepared to use the sister who loves him as a pawn, and even a sacrifice, if it will further his own ends. Although Tom and Louisa have received an identical upbringing, there is an important difference between them, since Louisa's interest in and sympathy for Sissy show that she is not wholly motivated by self-interest. As in the earlier scene in the schoolroom (Chapter 2), there is an effective irony in Sissy's failure to satisfy her teachers, since she is actually wiser than they – with a wisdom that is of the heart rather than the head, and that derives from her intuitions and spontaneous impulses rather than from logic or calculation. For instance, she ventures to question Mr M'Choakumchild's optimistic assumption (characteristic of the period) that an increase in national wealth means an increase in well-being for all: as Sissy points out, this only follows if the wealth is distributed equally, which is certainly not the case in Coketown. Mr M'Choakumchild has complete faith in statistics, as relating, for example, to fatal accidents. but Sissy sees the human realities that lie behind the figures – as she points out, it is no consolation to a bereaved person to know that the loved one who has been killed is part of a small percentage.

Summary

I,10. A new area of interest at a different social level is now opened up. The factory-worker Stephen Blackpool, forty years old but looking older on account of his life of toil and anxiety, is introduced, as is his friend Rachael, a neat, quiet woman of thirty-five who is also a factory hand. He speaks to her with obvious affection, but is obviously depressed, and his recurring phrase 'awlus a muddle' appears. When Stephen goes to his lodgings he finds that his wife, a slatternly drunkard whom he has not seen for some time, has returned to plague him. She is a degraded, almost subhuman creature, and there is later a hint that she has become a prostitute in order to obtain money for drink.

Commentary

Dickens's portrait of Stephen as a dignified, patient, industrious working-man is somewhat idealised; at the same time the novelist has attempted to give authenticity to the portrait by making Stephen speak in a broad northern dialect (for further discussion of this point, see p. 63). Stephen is the victim of a double tragedy: not only is he exploited in his working life by Bounderby, the owner of the mill, who grows rich while his workers can hardly keep body and soul together, but his private life is poisoned by the marriage in which he is trapped. This second point will be developed in later chapters. There is an obvious dramatic contrast between the two women in Stephen's life, and pathos in the fact that he cannot marry the one who loves him and would undoubtedly make him a good wife.

Summary

I,11. Following on (in the next instalment of the serial) from the previous chapter, Dickens shows us Stephen at work. During the dinner-hour he visits Bounderby to ask advice on how he can 'be ridded' of his wife. Bounderby tells him, uncompromisingly and unsympathetically, that it is impossible: divorce costs 'a mint of money' and is a luxury reserved for the rich.

Commentary

Stephen's hopes that he might be able to divorce his wife, and terminate the union that has long ago ceased to be a marriage in any except a legal sense, are dashed. This has the effect of intensifying his tragic predicament sketched in the previous chapter. Bounderby's undisguised contempt for his workers and his cynicism concerning Stephen's motives reveal the gulf that exists between what Benjamin Disraeli, popular novelist and later Prime Minister, called the 'two nations' in England, the rich and the poor: in practice if not in theory, there are plainly different laws for these two classes of citizens, and Dickens's choice of divorce to illustrate this disparity is an effective one. (For details on this point, see p. 55 below.)

Summary

I,12. When Stephen leaves Bounderby's house, a mysterious old woman who has evidently come to Coketown from the country asks him how Bounderby is and tells Stephen that she comes to town once a year. Working at his machine once again, Stephen reflects on the failure of his visit to Bounderby and is melancholy at the thought that he and Rachael cannot find happiness in marriage.

Commentary

The old woman adds to the plot-interest and is a figure of mystery whose full identity will only be revealed nineteen chapters later – though the shrewd reader may have his suspicions long before this point.

Summary

I,13. Stephen returns to his lodgings and finds Rachael nursing his wife, who is ill and delirious. The sick woman attempts to poison herself, but is prevented by Rachael; and Stephen realises with horror that he has been tempted to solve his problems by bringing about his wife's death – and indeed might have done so, depressed as he is by the discouraging news he has had from Bounderby, had it not been for Rachael's intervention.

Commentary

At one point Stephen says to Rachael, 'Thou art an Angel', and it is in this superhuman or at least saintly role that Rachael appears in this episode. Like the Good Samaritan in Christ's parable, she shows love and concern for one whom she has no particular reason to feel affection for and indeed might be supposed to have reason to hate. Unlike her social betters, Rachael shows a genuine spirit of Christianity.

Summary

I,14. After four chapters devoted to Stephen Blackpool, we return to the Gradgrind - Bounderby centre of interest. Some time has passed since we last saw them. Tom has entered Bounderby's bank as a junior clerk; Sissy has left school; and Gradgrind realises that Louisa is 'Quite a young woman'. Tom, who is as usual intent upon his own interest, reminds his sister that she can be useful to him and show that she really loves him. He does not explain in so many words how she can do this, but he clearly means by marrying Bounderby.

Commentary

We see Louisa moving towards a marriage that will certainly be loveless and may turn out to be disastrous, impelled by her brother's emotional blackmail combined with her own indifference as to her fate. Dickens is here gathering up threads of interest that have been apparent from as early as Chapter 4, and this chapter leads straight into the two that follow, which bring the development of this phase of the plot to a climax.

Summary

I,15. An interview takes place between Gradgrind and his daughter, in which she is informed that he has received an offer of marriage for her from Bounderby. From the worldly point of view it is a good match, but the disparity in years and temperament, and especially Louisa's manifest indifference towards (if not indeed dislike for) her prospective husband, do not promise much happiness. When Louisa asks her father three questions – 'do you think I love Mr Bounderby?'; 'do you ask me to love Mr Bounderby?'; 'does Mr Bounderby ask me to love him?' – he prevaricates. At last, without any enthusiasm, she agrees to marry him. Mrs Gradgrind is told the news; and when Sissy hears it she looks at Louisa with 'wonder', 'pity' and 'sorrow', whereupon Louisa's manner to her becomes suddenly cold and distant.

Commentary

This important scene is paralleled by another crucial interview between Louisa and her father thirteen chapters later, near the end of Book II (II,12). Although Gradgrind is not a bad father, he is a misguided one, and he is guilty of moral dishonesty in not facing up to the truth about Louisa's lack of feeling or respect for Bounderby. Alongside the dramatic dialogue is a pattern of imagery relating to smoke and fire (for further comments on this imagery in the novel as a whole, see p. 64). Near the beginning of the chapter, Louisa looks through the window at the high chimneys of Coketown with their 'long tracts of smoke'; later we are reminded that the distant smoke is 'very black and heavy'; and later still, Louisa tells her father, with apparent irrelevance, 'Yet when the night comes, Fire bursts out, father!' The black smoke, gloomy and funereal, seems to match Louisa's mood; and the observation that fire sometimes bursts forth foreshadows her own subsequent rebellion against the role of submission and passivity into which she is being cast: it is as if the fires of her heart, now banked up and showing no flame, will at some future date 'burst out'.

Summary

I,16. Bounderby breaks the news of his impending marriage to Mrs Sparsit, who agrees to move out of his home and live at the bank, where she will serve as a caretaker. Eight weeks after Louisa has agreed to marry Bounderby, the wedding takes place and the couple go to France for their honeymoon – not for any romantic reason, but because Bounderby wants to study the factory system in Lyons. The chapter ends with Tom's pleasure that his sister now occupies a situation in which she can be very useful to him, and with Louisa showing signs of awareness that she has taken a disastrously wrong step ('a little shaken in her reserved composure for the first time').

Commentary

The marriage forms the conclusion and climax of the first 'Book' of the novel; its results will be explored in the second 'Book'. We may deduce that Mrs Sparsit has herself had matrimonial designs upon Bounderby, and is therefore not a little put out when she learns he is to marry Louisa. This provides Mrs Sparsit with a motive for her behaviour in the ensuing chapters: she has a grudge against Louisa and devotes herself to trying to detect and expose her in some misbehaviour, as a balm for her own jealousy and resentment.

Summary

II,1. Mrs Sparsit is installed at the bank, where Bitzer is also employed as a porter (and, unofficially, as 'general spy and informer'). Bitzer describes Tom to Mrs Sparsit as 'a dissipated, extravagant idler'. A visitor arrives at the bank, armed with a letter of introduction to Bounderby from Mr Gradgrind, whom he has met in London. When the visitor learns that Gradgrind has married a very young girl, he shows signs of interest.

Commentary

Three points that are to have far-reaching consequences are made in this chapter. Tom's sinking into bad habits is both an indictment of the upbringing he has received and the cause of the crime he later commits. Bitzer is in sharp contrast to Tom, being 'an extremely clear-headed, cautious, prudent young man, who was safe to rise in the world': he is thus, from the point of view of Mr Gradgrind's educational theories, a successful product of the system; but the further comment that 'he had no affections or passions' warns us that something is missing in his nature and looks forward to the scene near the end of the book in which he is prepared to betray Tom. A new focus of interest appears in the person of the stranger, soon to be identified as James Harthouse. He is ironically described as 'a thorough gentleman' and represents Dickens's satire on the bored and effete privileged class: he has no real purpose in life and is entering politics not because he is eager to help run the country wisely, but in a half-hearted attempt to relieve his boredom. His interest in Louisa before he has even set eyes on her suggests that he is prepared to regard even a married woman as fair game in his rather languorous attempt to give variety to a life that is without purpose. To Dickens, who believed passionately in hard work and self-help, such an attitude was not merely immoral but despicable. Note that while the social world of *Hard Times* is almost entirely provincial and indeed northern, Harthouse represents a metropolitan upper class that Dickens identifies with parasitism: among the workers of Coketown (both factory hands like Stephen Blackpool and capitalists like Bounderby) this member of the 'idle rich' is like a fish out of water.

Summary

II,2. The stranger is named as James Harthouse, the younger brother of an M.P. He meets Bounderby and Louisa, tours the town with Bounderby and dines at his home. Louisa's coldness and indifference, rather than discouraging his attentions, only intrigue him the more; and he notices that Louisa shows unmistakable signs of animation when her brother appears. He therefore devotes himself to paying attention to Tom as a means of winning Louisa's favour.

Summary

II,3. A conversation takes place between Harthouse and Tom, in which the latter discloses that Louisa does not love Bounderby and only married him in order to secure advantages for her brother.

Commentary

These two chapters show Harthouse's developing interest in Louisa: learning that she does not love her husband, Harthouse conceives the idea of conducting an affair with her. He is not, of course, prompted by any real love for Louisa but takes her up, as he has taken up politics, in the hope of relieving his boredom. The ground is thus laid for important developments in the action – developments foreshadowed in the final paragraph of II,3, in which the reader is made aware that Tom's disclosures will have far-reaching effects.

Summary

II,4. For the next three chapters, attention reverts to Stephen Blackpool. In this chapter, a trade union agitator, Slackbridge, addresses a meeting of factory-workers concerning the case of Stephen, who has refused to join the union on account of a promise he made to Rachael not to become involved in possible trouble. Stephen defends himself against Slackbridge's attack, but with no success; for the meeting agrees that he will be sent to Coventry (i.e. ostracised by his fellow-workers, who will henceforth refuse to speak to him). At the end of the chapter, Stephen is sent for by Bounderby.

Commentary

Although Dickens's sympathies lie with the victims of the factory-system, he has little enthusiasm for the trades unions (see p. 53 for further discussion of this point), and Slackbridge is depicted as a somewhat ruthless mob-operator. The decision of the meeting has the effect of adding to Stephen's burden, since not only his private life but his working life is now a source of unhappiness to him. The isolation imposed upon him leads to 'the loneliest of lives, the life of solitude among a familiar crowd'.

Summary

II,5. At Bounderby's house, Stephen defends his fellow-workers against Bounderby's attack upon them: although he has been badly treated, he shows no resentment or ill-will. Bounderby accuses him of being a trouble-maker and gives him notice to leave the factory. Stephen knows that, having been dismissed from his job, he will find it very hard to obtain another.

Commentary

Stephen's Christian and almost saintly nature is shown in the compassion he feels for the fellow-workers who have rejected him, and in his readiness to explain their plight and defend their interests. At the same time, there is nothing passive about Stephen, who, rather than meekly bowing under Bounderby's blustering harshness, answers him at length, expounding the misery consequent upon the factory system and insisting that short-term measures such as transporting agitators like Slackbridge will not get to the root of the problem. Although he has had little education, Stephen has an unerring instinctive sense for what is right (resembling, in this respect, Sissy Jupe), and his long dialect speeches have an eloquence that stems from convictions.

Summary

II,6. As he leaves Bounderby's house, Stephen again meets the mysterious old woman who appeared in I,12. This time she is in the company of Rachael. She explains that she has heard of Bounderby's marriage and is anxious to catch a glimpse of his young wife. Stephen breaks the news to Rachael that he has lost his job and must therefore leave Coketown in search of work elsewhere. He invites the old lady to his lodgings and learns that she is a widow named Mrs Pegler. When her husband is mentioned, she shows signs of nervousness; she also discloses that she once had a son but has 'lost him'. Louisa and Tom arrive, and Mrs Pegler shows signs of alarm at the mention of the name Bounderby, apparently because she thinks that Bounderby has also come. Louisa offers to help Stephen, and he accepts two pounds from her (she has offered him more) but insists that it is to be regarded as a loan. Showing signs of excitement, Tom takes Stephen aside and, without giving any details, tells him he will do him 'a good turn': Stephen is to 'hang about the Bank' for an hour each evening until his departure. Stephen bids farewell to Rachael, both of them judging it better that she should not be seen with him again lest similar trouble fall upon her. During the next few days, he completes the work on which he is engaged at the factory; after work each evening, he loiters outside the bank as Tom has instructed him, without understanding what purpose it will serve.

Commentary

This is an important chapter in the development of the action and involves 'plotting' in two senses: Dickens the novelist is ingeniously preparing for later events, and Tom is hatching his own plot. (Even Mrs Pegler might be regarded as the author of a mystery story.) The reappearance of Mrs Pegler underlines the parallel between II,5 and I,12, the two scenes in which Stephen visits Mr Bounderby's house: in the earlier scene Bounderby callously told him that there was no hope for him of finding happiness through remarriage; in the later scene Bounderby, equally callously, turned away a good worker who had the courage – or audacity – to think for himself. The mystery of Mrs Pegler increases, though some readers, alerted by the ambiguous reference to a 'lost' son as well as by her obvious interest in Bounderby, will feel that they have solved it by now. The appearance of Tom and Louisa in Blackpool's lodgings is a mild coincidence that is necessary in order to show us Mrs Pegler's reactions. Louisa's sympathy for Stephen and her desire to help him show that, for all her upbringing, her heart is not without compassion. Tom's instructions to Stephen indicate that he has already formed the idea of robbing the bank and throwing the blame on Stephen: evidently the idea of using Stephen as a scapegoat has been quickly formed, for he can only just have learned that Stephen is to leave Coketown and will be suspected of harbouring some grudge against Bounderby.

Summary

II,7. The significance of the chapter-title, 'Gunpowder', becomes clear only when we reach the next chapter, 'Explosion'. Harthouse now spends a good deal of his time with Louisa during her husband's absence, and is more and more attracted to her. For her part, she shows only coldness towards him; but he perseveres, seeking to win her favour by appealing to her love for Tom. He tells her that Tom has been losing money at gambling, and Louisa admits that she has lent him 'a considerable sum'. Harthouse offers to try to persuade Tom to mend his ways, and subsequently has a conversation with Tom, who shows resentment that Louisa has not provided him with more money and insists that she could have obtained it from Bounderby if she had really tried. When Harthouse happens to use the word 'banker', Tom suddenly turns pale and is evidently disturbed. He tells Harthouse that it is now too late for any loan to be of use to him. Harthouse asks him to show more affection towards his sister; and when Tom next sees Louisa he speaks to her more tenderly – whereupon she smiles at Harthouse, recognising that this is his doing.

Commentary

By this point in the action, both Tom and Louisa are now separately moving towards the climax of their separate lines of action. Tom's predicament is clearly reaching a crisis, though there is an element of mystery as to what he is planning to do: his turning pale at the mention of the word 'banker' is a clue that the skilful reader may be able to interpret. (As a generalisation, it may be said that Dickens likes to create his effects dramatically rather than analytically: in other words, we are given no insight into the secret workings of Tom's mind, but we hear his speech and witness the visible signs of his behaviour just as we might do in watching a play; and it is from this evidence that we must construct a hypothesis as to the state of his mind and its causes and possible results.) Louisa, too, is becoming more entangled in a relationship with Harthouse, who quite consciously exploits her affection for Tom in order to make her grateful to him and thus to deepen the intimacy between them.

Summary

II,8. The chapter begins by summing up the development of Harthouse's relationship with Louisa up to this point in the action (it is relevant that this chapter formed a separate weekly instalment, so that the reader might need reminding of the state of affairs prevailing when the previous portion of the story broke off). The narrator comments that Harthouse has no premeditated 'wickedness of purpose' – in plain English, he has not set out deliberately to seduce Louisa – but is merely 'indifferent and purposeless', giving no thought to the implications or possible results of his conduct. Bounderby tells him that the bank has been robbed of a relatively small sum taken from the safe that is in Tom's keeping, and also mentions that Louisa fainted when she heard the news. Bounderby suspects Stephen Blackpool, who has been observed lurking about the bank; an old woman has also been seen in suspicious circumstances. Louisa asks Tom whether he has anything to tell her; he refuses to take the opportunity to confide in her, but after she has left him he shows signs of great distress. Mr Bounderby moves Mrs Sparsit temporarily into his home.

Commentary

The 'gunpowder' that has now 'exploded' (see the comment on the chapter-titles under II,7) is Tom's plan to steal from Bounderby and to lay the blame on Stephen: the image is of a store of gunpowder, potentially dangerous, that is at last ignited, and it thus forms part of the cluster of fire-images so prominent in this novel. Bounderby's suspicions of Stephen are readily arrived at, since they confirm his earlier prejudices; Louisa's reaction to the news, on the other hand, suggests that she suspects the truth, and her attempt to encourage Tom to confide in her points in the same direction. The references to Harthouse in the early part of this chapter remind us that, at this stage of the action, Dickens is simultaneously pursuing several narrative lines – not only Tom's crime and Stephen's unwitting involvement in it, but also Harthouse's act of sabotage (to pursue the 'gunpowder' image) directed at Louisa's marriage.

Summary

II,9. Mrs Sparsit, aware of the growing intimacy between Louisa and Harthouse, ingratiates herself with Bounderby, flattering him and bestowing upon him special acts of attention that emphasise his wife's indifference. As a result, Louisa's 'dangerous alienation from her husband' increases as relations between them become more openly hostile. News arrives that Mrs Gradgrind is dying, and Louisa arrives in time to witness her death.

Commentary

Mrs Sparsit's role as spy and plotter against Louisa and Harthouse is to
be prominent from this point onwards; her motives have been made
clear much earlier, in her chagrin at being disappointed of securing
Gradgrind as a husband herself. Exactly why Dickens kills off Mrs
Gradgrind at this point is not immediately clear; but a clue can be
found in her deathbed speech to Louisa, which shows more eloquence
and understanding (even if only a half-formed understanding) than she
has ever shown in her lifetime. She tells Louisa that 'there is something . . . that your father has missed, or forgotten'; and this reminds us
that the results of Mr Gradgrind's experiment in education is now
before our eyes in the shape of Tom's crime and Louisa's unhappy
marriage and entanglement with Harthouse. Mrs Gradgrind thus evinces
the truth-telling traditionally associated with the dying; and although
she has been a figure of fun during her lifetime, the reference to her
passing at the end of the chapter has an impressive and moving solemnity
reinforced by the allusion to the form of service for the burial of the
dead in the Book of Common Prayer of the Church of England.

Summary

II,10. Mrs Sparsit continues her clandestine activities as a spy upon
Louisa and Harthouse. The bank robbery remains unsolved, Louisa tells
Harthouse that she cannot believe that Stephen is guilty, but he
attempts to persuade her that it is likely.

Commentary

Again, Dickens is keeping two main interests going in this chapter; the
progress of Louisa's liaison with Harthouse, and the mystery of who
robbed the bank. The chapter-title is 'Mrs Sparsit's Staircase', and the
image of the staircase which Louisa is metaphorically descending, to
meet ruin and disaster at the bottom, is reiterated in the titles of the
next two chapters ('Lower and Lower' and 'Down'). The appropriateness of the image consists in the idea it conveys of a steady, relentless
progression towards the 'dark pit of shame and ruin at the bottom' –
that is, Louisa's apparently inevitable elopement and adultery. Louisa's
sympathy for Stephen, and her true reading of his character, are contrasted with Harthouse's negligent cynicism.

Summary

II,11. Mrs Sparsit learns from Tom that Harthouse, who has been absent for a short time 'shooting in Yorkshire', is due to arrive back in Coketown during Bounderby's absence in London and has asked Tom to meet him at the station. She installs herself at the station as a spy; but when Harthouse fails to arrive she realises that this is a trick on Harthouse's part, designed to keep Tom out of the way, and she dashes to Bounderby's house some way out of Coketown. There she finds Harthouse has already joined Louisa, and she spies on them both in a wood. Although Louisa asks Harthouse to leave her, he declares his love for her; they arrange to meet again 'that night', presumably to go away together, and Harthouse rides off in a terrific thunderstorm that drenches the unfortunate Mrs Sparsit to the skin. Notwithstanding her acute (and highly comical) discomfort, she follows Louisa to Coketown; but when the train on which they are both travelling reaches the station, she loses her.

Commentary

This chapter is the middle one of the three that form the climax of the second 'Book' of the novel and are linked by the image of the staircase as well as by the developing action. It ends, so to speak, on a question mark: where has Louisa gone? The obvious assumption is that she has eluded Mrs Sparsit, wittingly or unwittingly, and has gone to meet Harthouse, who has evidently been doing some plotting on his own account, since his device to keep Tom out of the way is part of a premeditated scheme. Mrs Sparsit is cast in the role of a comic detective, motivated by spite and envy; and she too has been carrying out a plot of her own devising. There is thus a wealth of plotting in both senses of the term.

Summary

II,12. Mr Gradgrind is shown at home. His daughter Louisa arrives unexpectedly, tells him how unhappy she has been in her marriage, confesses to him that Harthouse has made a declaration of love to her, assures him that 'I have not disgraced you', and ends by falling unconscious at his feet.

Commentary

Louisa's action in returning to her old home and telling her father the truth represents a 'reversal' of the action: the reader who has expected her to run away with Harthouse finds that – contrary to the assumptions of both Harthouse and Mrs Sparsit – she is not prepared to take such an irrevocable step, but, for all her unhappiness and desperation, retains a sense of right behaviour. This is the climax of Louisa's role in the novel; it also represents the failure of Harthouse's irresponsible schemings and a humiliating disappointment for him; and, most important of all, it brings home to Mr Gradgrind the utter failure of his system of education. This is the note on which the chapter emphatically ends, with Gradgrind observing 'the pride of his heart and the triumph of his system, lying, an insensible heap, at his feet'. But it is not, of course, the end of the novel, since the fate of that other important victim of the Gradgrind system, Tom, is still undetermined, and the bank robbery remains unsolved, Stephen Blackpool still lying under the cloud of suspicion. These matters remain to be cleared up in the third and shortest 'Book' of the novel. In the present chapter, the dialogue between Louisa and her father carries most of the burden of meaning; or, to put it another way, Dickens has conceived and written the scene very much in terms of the stage. Louisa's dialogue in particular is distinctly stagey (e.g. 'I curse the hour in which I was born to such a destiny'). The scene forms a parallel or complement to that which occurred near the end of the first 'Book' (I,15) and showed the interview between father and daughter in which she agreed, far from enthusiastically, to marry Bounderby.

Summary

III,1. Mr Gradgrind begins to show signs of rejecting his former convictions: schooled by suffering, he realises that he is largely responsible for Louisa's present misery and the plight in which she finds herself. In one of the most important passages of the novel, he admits that there may after all be something in the belief that there is 'a wisdom of the Heart' as well as 'a wisdom of the Head'. Sissy offers her help and comfort to Louisa, who, after some resistance, abandons her attitude of coldness and pride and accepts Sissy's friendship.

Commentary

In this chapter Dickens begins to demonstrate the effects of the scene that has been related in II,12. A fundamental change is beginning to take place in Mr Gradgrind: hitherto scornful of 'the wisdom of the Heart', he now cannot ignore the damage that his doctrines have done to his beloved daughter's life and happiness. The appearance of Sissy at this point is significant, for it is she who – through her associations with the circus as well as through her own nature – has throughout the novel embodied 'the wisdom of the Heart'. When Louisa, at the end of the chapter, falls upon her knees and 'clinging to *this stroller's child* looked up at her almost with veneration' (my italics), the social roles are strikingly reversed: Dickens reminds us that, despite Sissy's humble origins and her lowly position in the Gradgrind household, she is Louisa's superior in natural goodness and moral insight, and worthy to act as her mentor or exemplar.

Summary

III.2. Harthouse is perplexed by Louisa's failure to keep their assignation, since he knows nothing as yet concerning her change of heart. Sissy visits him, tells him that he must not expect ever to speak to Louisa again, and asks him to leave the neighbourhood at once. After protesting that to do so will make him appear ridiculous, since he is supposedly in Coketown on political business, he agrees and decides to escape the situation by going abroad.

Commentary

Harthouse is not really a villain, since weakness rather than evil is at the root of his nature and his actions. But Dickens's principle of a fair distribution of rewards and punishments at the end of the novel requires that he shall at least be humiliated and rejected; and it is significant that the agent employed is again Sissy. As in the previous chapter, the 'stroller's child' shows herself to be the moral superior of the fine gentleman. The humiliating irony of his 'defeat' by one who, from his point of view, belongs to the dregs of society is not lost on Harthouse, who reflects, after Sissy has left him: 'Only a poor girl – only a stroller – only James Harthouse made nothing of – only James Harthouse a Great Pyramid of failure.'

Summary

III,3. Mrs Sparsit goes to London and tells Bounderby what she believes has happened: that Louisa and Harthouse have run away together. (She is of course wrong in this assumption, but does not yet realise it.) Bounderby returns at once to Coketown and is astonished to learn that Louisa is at her father's house. When Mr Gradgrind suggests that it would be better for her to remain there for a time, Bounderby delivers an ultimatum: if she does not return to the matrimonial home by the next day, she had better not return at all. The following day, Louisa having failed to return to him, he sends her belongings to her father's house and resumes 'a bachelor life'.

Commentary

The narrative of Mrs Sparsit's actions continues at the point at which it left off in II,11, her eagerness to make trouble between Louisa and her husband leading her to assume that the worst has happened, even though she has no positive evidence. Bounderby's rejection of Louisa is entirely in character and effectively terminates their disastrous relationship.

Summary

III,4. Bounderby renews his efforts to solve the mystery of the bank robbery and offers a reward of twenty pounds for the arrest of Stephen Blackpool, whom he still believes to be guilty. Slackbridge makes a speech denouncing Stephen as a thief and a fugitive from justice. Mr Bounderby, Tom and Rachael call on Louisa, who confirms Rachael's story (which Bounderby has so far refused to believe) that she and her brother visited Stephen's lodgings and that she gave money to Stephen out of a feeling of compassion (see II,6). Rachael states that she has written to Stephen, who is living at a distance from Coketown, urging him to return in order to clear his name; and she promises that he will be there within two days. However, Stephen fails to arrive, and it is generally believed that he has been warned by Rachael and has made his escape. Tom, who has been in a state of great agitation, gains confidence when Stephen fails to appear.

Commentary

After devoting a considerable amount of space to the Louisa–Bounderby–Harthouse story, Dickens now returns to the part of his narrative that is concerned with Stephen, Tom and the bank robbery. This chapter raises but does not answer a question: what has happened to Stephen? The reader's knowledge of his character makes it unlikely that he has run away to save his skin; but we have to wait another two chapters (in the case of the original readers of the serial, another week) to have the mystery solved.

Summary

III,5. Rachael and Sissy speculate on what can have happened to Stephen. Meanwhile, Mrs Sparsit has tracked down and seized Mrs Pegler, whom she believes to be an accomplice in the crime, and takes her to Bounderby's house. Instead of being pleased, Bounderby is infuriated and turns on Mrs Sparsit. Mrs Pegler discloses that she is Bounderby's mother, and it emerges that all his oft-repeated stories of the ill treatment he was subjected to as a child and his early struggles are a pack of lies: he has in fact had a loving and respectable upbringing, which he has repaid with ingratitude. Knowing that soon the truth will have spread all over Coketown, Bounderby is humiliated. The chapter ends with a reminder that Stephen is still missing and with Louisa's fear, shared by Sissy, that Tom may be guilty of a worse crime than theft: that he may have murdered Stephen in order to prevent his reappearance, which might result in the truth emerging.

Commentary

The chapter begins and ends by maintaining the reader's suspense and curiosity as to the fate of Stephen Blackpool. The main action of the chapter concerns the 'discovery' of two hidden but related truths: that the mysterious Mrs Pegler is (as the reader may well already have guessed) Bounderby's mother, and that his inverted snobbery, which has led him to boast of his childhood misery, has no foundation in fact. Once again, Mrs Sparsit's plot has misfired: hoping to win her employer's favour and gratitude, she has accomplished exactly the opposite. Since Bounderby and Mrs Sparsit are, in their different ways, both highly unsympathetic characters, their respective discomfiture is welcomed. Note that Bounderby, like Harthouse a little earlier, suffers humiliation: the implication is that, for a time at least, he will be the laughing-stock of Coketown.

Summary

III,6. Sissy and Rachael take a walk in the country near Coketown. The narrative includes a reference to disused mines in the area which are a source of danger to the unwary walker. They discover Stephen's hat, then realise that he has fallen down a mine-shaft known locally as Old Hell Shaft. Sissy runs back to the town for help, and a man is lowered down the shaft. He reports that Stephen is alive but is seriously injured. At last he is brought to the surface; after making a speech about the way in which he has met his death, he asks that his name be cleared and says that Tom can provide an explanation. Stephen then dies.

Commentary

Again, Dickens makes use of a coincidence that is not likely to trouble the reader who is being carried along by the power of the narrative: it is, to say the least, lucky that Sissy and Rachael should stumble on the dying Stephen in this way, but the horror of the discovery and the excitement of the rescue attempt are vividly conveyed. There is a symbolic appropriateness in the way in which Stephen meets his death: as he points out in his lengthy speeches (a little implausible, in strictly realistic terms, for a dying man – but Dickens's art is not a wholly realistic one), the mine-shaft has caused the death of many while it was being worked, and even though it is in operation no longer it still claims men's lives. Stephen, who has been a victim of the industrial system during his lifetime, dies a victim of the same callous exploitation and indifference to human life and safety. It is important to note that this is not a natural hazard but the result of greed and indifference: from the legislators in London (like Mr Gradgrind) to the local capitalists (like Bounderby), no one has thought it worth while spending a little money to render the mine safe. Stephen's favourite expression, 'Awlus a muddle!', recurs like a refrain throughout his dying speeches. This chapter clears up the mystery of what has become of Stephen, but the final portion reminds us that Tom has still not been brought to book and points forward to the resolution of this part of the story, to be effected in the next two chapters.

Summary

III,7. Knowing that he will now be sought for and questioned, with the help of Sissy Tom makes his escape. Mr Gradgrind realises that his son is guilty and learns from Louisa that he is in hiding at Mr Sleary's circus at some considerable distance from Coketown, having been sent there by the resourceful Sissy. They set off and at last catch up with the circus, where they learn that Tom is still safe. When Gradgrind confronts his son and asks him sorrowfully why he committed the crime, Tom answers him in terms that have been learned in the Gradgrind school of 'hard facts': statistically speaking, out of a given number of employees, a certain proportion will inevitably turn out to be dishonest. Tom disclaims personal responsibility for his conduct ('How can I help laws?' – that is, generalisations based on the observation of human behaviour in the mass). Tom is told that he must be conveyed to Liverpool and smuggled abroad, where he will be beyond the reach of the law; but at this point Bitzer arrives, seizes Tom, and announces that he intends to hand him over to justice.

Commentary

In a very striking and effective way, Dickens in this chapter returns to and brings together some of the main motifs from the opening chapters of the novel: the Gradgrind philosophy of calculation and self-interest (by now largely abandoned by Mr Gradgrind himself, but still very much in evidence in the motives of Tom and Bitzer); Sissy and Bitzer as representatives of contrasting systems of values; and the circus, especially through its proprietor and spokesman Sleary, as an institution standing at the furthest possible point from the utilitarian principles of Coketown. Tom's guilt, though not formally proved, is now generally acknowledged by those closest to him – including his father, for whom, coming on top of the breakdown of Louisa's marriage, it is a culminating proof of the failure of his educational methods. The attempt to save Tom is threatened by Bitzer, and the chapter ends with the reader left in suspense as to whether Bitzer's counter-plot will succeed. Dramatically speaking, there are some very telling moments in this chapter. One occurs when Mr Gradgrind, 'forlorn', sits down 'on the Clown's performing chair in the middle of the ring': we remember his earlier disapproval of his children's interest in the circus, and it comes home to us how far Mr Gradgrind has travelled that he should now implicitly be accepting the values of the circus (as, in practical terms, he has been glad to accept Mr Sleary's help and advice). Another such moment occurs when Tom, the product of the Gradgrind system, is ludicrously attired in clown's costume as a disguise: Dickens is inviting us to witness what is, almost literally, a transformation scene. When Tom, rather than showing remorse or repentance, answers his father in terms that he himself has taught, Mr Gradgrind cannot escape the realisation that he is ultimately responsible for what has happened: 'I have heard you talk, a hundred times, of its being a law. . . . You have comforted others with such things, father. Comfort yourself!'

Summary

III,8. Gradgrind pleads with Bitzer to show compassion for Tom and gratitude towards himself; but Bitzer is adamant, responding only in the terms that he has learned in the Gradgrind school. With the help of Sleary and the circus animals, however, Bitzer is outwitted and Tom makes his escape. Sleary tells Gradgrind that he has evidence that Sissy's father is dead, but recommends that she should not be told, since the reason for his abandoning her can now never be known.

Commentary

By a double twist in the action, Bitzer, who had sought to cheat the attempt to rescue Tom, is himself cheated. It is a brilliant stroke on Dickens's part that this should be largely accomplished through the circus animals, the horses and dogs: those creatures of instinct, unquestioning in their loyalty, stand at the opposite pole from the self-seeking, calculating attitude of Bitzer. (This point comes to the surface of the text when, in response to Sleary's observation that 'dogth ith wonderful animalth', Gradgrind replies – without fully appreciating the significance of his reply – that 'Their instinct . . . is surprising'. 'Instinct' is not a word, or a concept, that he has been in the habit of using.) As in his conversation with Tom in the previous chapter, Gradgrind is once again forced to confront the fact that he is being repaid in his own coin: when he sorrowfully asks Bitzer whether he has a heart, that former model pupil replies in terms that would have won him approval in the Gradgrind school ('the circulation . . . couldn't be carried on without one'). The reference to Sissy's father ties up a thread in the plot that would otherwise be left hanging loose.

Commentary

III,9. In this final chapter, Dickens winds up his story by disposing of his major characters with some indication of their various fates – the novelist in effect performing the function of Providence in doling out appropriate rewards and punishments. Her various plots having all misfired, Mrs Sparsit is dismissed from Bounderby's service. Bitzer takes

Tom's place in the bank. Tom goes into exile, presumably somewhere in the colonies, that favourite dumping-ground for ne'er-do-wells, repents of his misdeeds and dies young. (This fulfils Dickens's moral scheme: although Tom has been allowed to escape, he does not really deserve being let off so lightly, since his offences – not merely the robbery but the heartless attempt to incriminate Stephen – have been heinous.) Stephen is posthumously exonerated. Rachael continues her life of lonely toil, showing pity for Stephen's drunken wife when the opportunity arises. Sissy marries, has children and lives a life of happy usefulness. Louisa, on the other hand, finds no such fulfilment, her life having, like her brother's, been permanently blighted by her experiences. Mr Gradgrind, who may perhaps be regarded as the protagonist if not actually the hero of the novel, is a reformed character, having seen the error of his ways and rejected the doctrines formerly associated with his name.

3 THEMES AND ISSUES

Some of Dickens's novels, such as *Great Expectations*, are partly or wholly set in an earlier period; but *Hard Times* is very much a topical novel – the full title of the first edition (1854), indeed, was *Hard Times. For These Times* – and the issues it presents were in the air when it was written. This chapter will explore major aspects of the most important questions with which the novel is concerned.

The main plot of *Hard Times* raises the question: what kind of education is best? ('education' in this context meaning the whole upbringing of the child, the influences to which it is exposed and the vaues that are inculcated, not merely what happens in school). Although we do not see or hear much of the Gradgrind school after the opening chapters, the initial setting in the school-room gives prominence to this theme; and the educational theme looms large in the presentation of such major characters as Gradgrind, Tom, Louisa, Sissy and Bitzer. The sub-plot concerns the Coketown factories and their workers, and the main representatives of what we may call the 'industrial' theme are Stephen and Rachael.

With great skill, born of nearly twenty years' experience as a novelist, Dickens links these two areas of the novel in numerous ways. Bounderby, for instance, is a friend of Gradgrind and eventually husband of Louisa, but is also a factory-owner and employer of Stephen, and is clearly a major link. Tom robs the bank and tries to place the blame on Stephen; Louisa shows her compassion for Stephen; and apart from these links through character and event, the unified setting of Coketown helps to bring the two themes closer together. (When Louisa talks to her father in I,15, for instance, she looks out of the window and sees the factory chimneys – a reminder that the two social worlds of the novel coexist in close proximity.)

This chapter, then, will be mainly concerned with the way in which Dickens expounds the 'educational' and 'industrial' themes of the novel, and the convictions he expresses. It will also deal, more briefly, with the minor theme of marriage and divorce which the novel touches on.

3.1 EDUCATION: THE HEAD AND THE HEART

In the novels that preceded *Hard Times*, Dickens had often written – usually critically and satirically – about schools and teachers: in *Nicholas Nickleby* (1839), for instance, he had attacked the boarding-schools run for profit by incompetent and sometimes brutal masters; in *Dombey and Son* (1848), he had poked gentler fun at the arid pretensions of an 'academy' for middle-class boys, with its irrelevant curriculum based on the dead languages; in *David Copperfield* (1850) he had included an account of his hero's schooldays. In *Hard Times*, however, the theme is more prominent, and more comprehensively dealt with, than ever before; and Dickens's range extends from specific questions such as teaching methods to be used in the classroom to fundamental matters of educational philosophy.

3.1(a) Mr Gradgrind

According to Philip Collins, whose *Dickens and Education* (1963) is a valuable study to which I am much indebted in this section, Gradgrind is, unlike most of Dickens's heroes, 'a man of ideas – ideas which he expresses through the school he has established'. The starting-point of the novel, in its very first sentence, is Gradgrind's faith in 'facts' as the sole basis of education and life; and a major strand of the novel is concerned with the practical outcome of his doctrines as applied to two of his children, Louisa and Tom. By the end of the novel, with his philosophy exposed as pernicious, Gradgrind has undergone a process of re-education and has rejected his former doctrines in favour of a more human faith in the feelings and the imagination.

The opposing sets of ideas are often referred to in the novel as 'fact' and 'fancy', though in III,1 they are also summed up in two memorable phrases: the 'wisdom of the Head' and the 'wisdom of the Heart'. The former places sole emphasis on reason, on precise knowledge of a scientific or factual kind, on the measurable and quantifiable, and on self-interest as a motive for effort. This system of values, cold and calculating, has sometimes been related to the ideas of the Utilitarians, an important group of nineteenth-century philosophers and political theorists who were inspired by the ideas of Jeremy Bentham (1748–1832) and whose later practitioners included James Mill (1773–1836) and his son John Stuart Mill (1806–73). It has even been suggested that Gradgrind's name may be a sly allusion to that of James Mill. However, to identify Gradgrind's views with those of the Utilitarians is unfair and misleading, since they did not advocate the adoption of 'utility' in the narrowest sense as a principle of political and social conduct.

When we first meet Gradgrind, he is addressing and questioning the children in the school he has established. (A system of compulsory state education did not come into effect until the year of Dickens's death, and at this period schools were maintained by private philanthropists or by various charitable and religious organisations.) With great economy and effectiveness, Dickens indicates the characteristics of the Gradgrind system: for Mr Gradgrind, Sissy is 'girl number twenty' and her father, who is a circus performer, 'a veterinary surgeon, a farrier, and horse-breaker'. This impulse to reduce complex and living human realities to arid categories is typical, and is also evinced in the request to 'define' a horse, which baffles Sissy but is efficiently complied with by Bitzer. This is, as Professor Collins notes, 'a parody of the object-lesson', a favourite teaching technique of the time, whereby some object would be shown, or simply mentioned, to the children, and a definition consisting of an accumulation of isolated facts couched in scientific language would be committed to memory. As Dickens makes clear, no child who does not know already what a horse is would be in the least enlightened by 'Quadruped. Graminivorous . . . ', etc., and no child who, like Sissy, knows and loves horses needs such an exclusively intellectual and verbal description.

Mr Gradgrind may be wrong-headed, however, but he is at least sincere and consistent in his beliefs; and we soon learn that his own middle-class children have been subjected to the same methods as the poorer children in the school – indeed, it has dominated their lives to the exclusion of everything else:

> No little Gradgrind had ever seen a face in the moon; it was up in the moon [i.e. instructed in astronomical knowledge] before it could speak distinctly. . . . (I,3)

The subsequent fortunes of Tom and Louisa show that the 'wisdom of the Head' is inadequate for human happiness: the starvation of their imagination and their capacity to feel emotion has the short-run effect of making them bored and discontented and the long-run effect of leading them to make serious mistakes in their moral conduct.

The titles that Dickens gave to the three 'Books' into which *Hard Times* is divided – 'Sowing', 'Reaping' and 'Garnering' – seem to refer to Mr Gradgrind and the effect of his doctrines. The allusion is to St Paul's text, 'Whatsoever a man soweth, that shall he also reap' (Galatians vi. 7); 'garnering', which means storing up grain for future use, continues the same metaphor. The education described in the first 'Book' has its results in the second, where Louisa's marriage comes to grief and Tom yields to temptation and first gambles and then becomes a thief.

3.1(b) Mr M'Choakumchild

Although Mr M'Choakumchild is referred to several times in the book, he appears only once, in the opening scene. He is an example of Dickens's *specific* as opposed to his *general* satire. Whereas, for instance, the whole mentality of the Gradgrind school of educational philosophy is attacked in general terms, M'Choakumchild is a representative of a particular body of people who were in the news at the time the novel was written. To quote Philip Collins:

> The first batch of Queen's Scholars, enlisted as pupil-teachers under Kay-Shuttleworth's 1846 Minutes, had emerged from the training colleges in 1853, and naturally their graduation and departure to the schools had renewed popular interest in the scheme.

Towards the end of I,2 we are told that M'Choakumchild and 'some one hundred and forty other schoolmasters had been lately turned at the same time, in the same factory, on the same principles, like so many pianoforte legs'. The description of the training college as a 'factory', and the comparison of the training to an industrial process such as producing machine-turned piano legs, are of course consistent with Dickens's presentation of the Gradgrind school as a soulless institution, mechanical in its methods and taking no account of human individuality.

This newly trained teacher has been stuffed with facts, which he regurgitates for his unfortunate pupils. Dickens's catalogue of the subjects covered in the college curriculum concentrates entirely on subjects in which rote-learning is at a premium. Of deeper understanding of the value and significance of what he has learned, there is no trace; nor is there any suggestion that it will be adapted to the particular needs of the children who come before him. The paragraph concludes: 'Ah, rather overdone, M'Choakumchild. If he had only learnt a little less, how infinitely better he might have taught much more!'

Professor Collins cites evidence to show that this portrait was not much exaggerated. A training college principal reported:

> The present course pursued in training schools tends to *impart information* rather than to *develop the faculties and to discipline the mind*. Vast demands are made on the memory, little is done for the improvement of the judgment or reasoning powers. . . . In such subjects as Old Testament history, Church history, outlines of English history, there is necessarily an immense preponderance of names, dates, and facts, which have to be *remembered* but not *digested*.

A school inspector suggested that 'it would be far better if you could get schoolmasters with less knowledge and more education' – which is exactly Dickens's point, but was made several years after Dickens had written *Hard Times*.

It has been suggested, quite persuasively, that the name M'Choakumchild is a comic allusion to that of J. M. M'Culloch, a Scottish educationist whose *Series of Lessons in Prose and Verse* (1831) was widely used as a school textbook. M'Culloch's claim that he had chosen the readings to impart 'knowledge of useful and interesting facts' is not far from the world of the novel; and his scornful reference in his preface to 'such preposterous and unsuitable exercises as enacting dramatic scenes, . . . and reading the latest sentimental poetry' recalls Mr Gradgrind's impatience with imaginative literature.

3.1(c) The government officer

In the schoolroom scene with which *Hard Times* opens, three adults are present: Mr Gradgrind, M'Choakumchild and an unnamed 'third gentleman' identified only as 'a government officer'. He never appears again or is referred to again in the novel, but he is of importance in this scene because his questioning of the class is reported at length. Like M'Choakumchild, the government officer is a good example of Dickens's specific satire on a contemporary institution whose doings were topical when the novel appeared.

As K. J. Fielding has shown in his essay, 'Charles Dickens and the Department of Practical Art' (*Modern Language Review*, 1953), Dickens clearly had in mind the Department of Practical Art established by the Board of Trade in 1852. The Great Exhibition of 1851 had revealed the weakness of British manufactures in industrial design, and the new department was intended to encourage good and discourage bad design in such commodities as carpets, wallpaper, pottery and textiles. Professor Fielding's conclusion is that 'it would be entirely wrong to accept Dickens's travesty as deserved': the officials of the Department, so far from being rigidly literal-minded, were quite reasonably concerned to improve standards of industrial design and to curb the wilder extravagances of Victorian bad taste. For some reason, however, Dickens depicts the government officer as an ally of Gradgrind, and makes him proclaim: ' "you are not to see anywhere what you don't see in fact; you are not to have anywhere what you don't have in fact" '.

Dickens had evidently read one of the lectures given by an official of the Department and published in 1853, shortly before he began work on *Hard Times*; and from this lecture he took material for the government officer's speeches. For example, the lecturer, Owen Jones, had said:

> Here are specimens of English papers, than which nothing can be more absurd, – a wall covered with repetitions of the same subject, men and horses standing on each other's heads, or steamers floating on each other's masts. . . . All direct representation of natural objects in paper-hangings should be avoided . . . because it places these objects in unseemly positions.

Again, speaking of calico-printing, he complained that in some designs

> We walk on flowers and tropical plants crushing beneath our feet. . . .

This provides the questions that Dickens puts in the official's mouth: ' "Would you paper a room with representations of horses? . . . Would you use a carpet having a representation of flowers upon it?" '

Henry Cole, the General Superintendent of the Department of Practical Art, was an acquaintance of Dickens and seems to have taken the satire on his work in good part. On 17 June 1854 Dickens wrote him a letter that acknowledges his 'good humour' and concludes with an interesting reference to the novel:

> I often say to Mr Gradgrind that there is reason and good intention in much that he does – in fact, in all that he does – but that he overdoes it. Perhaps by dint of his going his way and my going mine, we shall meet at last at some halfway house where there are flowers on the carpets, and a little standing-room for Queen Mab's Chariot among the Steam Engines.

That last phrase is another version of the antithesis of 'fancy' and 'fact' that is so important in the novel ('Queen Mab's Chariot' being a reference to Mercutio's famous speech in Shakespeare's *Romeo and Juliet*, where Queen Mab is 'the fairies' midwife' and the cause of dreams).

3.1(d) Louisa and Tom

Louisa and her brother are the guinea-pigs for Mr Gradgrind's experiment in rearing the young on an unrelieved diet of facts. When we first meet them in I,3, their childhood is already over (Louisa is 'fifteen or sixteen'), and the profoundly unsatisfactory results of their upbringing are already evident. That system of education is referred to in the fourth paragraph of the chapter:

> No little Gradgrind had ever associated a cow in a field with that famous cow who killed the rat who ate the malt, or with that yet more famous cow who swallowed Tom Thumb; it had never heard of those celebrities, and had only been introduced to a cow as a graminivorous ruminating quadruped with several stomachs.

The references are, of course, to the nursery rhyme 'The house that Jack built' and the folktale of Tom Thumb – these being examples of the kind of imaginative literature, opening up for the child a world of wonder and romance, that had been sternly prohibited in the Gradgrind family. The polysyllabic definition of a cow, on the other hand, typifies the scientific or pseudo-scientific nature of the Gradgrind system of education, with its jaw-breaking Latinisms utterly unintelligible to a child; it also recalls the 'definition of a horse' demanded of the children at the Gradgrind school in the previous chapter.

Although Dickens's tone in this passage is witty and ironical, he was not exaggerating the kind of approach that was thought suitable by many teachers and educational thinkers in this period, and the definitions of a cow and a horse can be paralleled in actual textbooks of the time. Philip Collins quotes from one called *The School and the Teacher*, published in 1857, which suggests that the children should be given some useful information concerning cats:

> Front teeth in each jaw, 6; canine teeth, 2 in each jaw, very powerful and formed for tearing; molar or cheek teeth, 4. . . . Feet formed for walking; toes on the fore feet, 5; – hind feet, 4. . . .

There is here the same emphasis on precise facts, and the same exclusion of feeling, that Dickens attributes to the examples connected with Gradgrind.

I,3 makes it clear that there is something missing in the Gradgrind system, since Louisa and Tom are unhappy and without purpose. That they should instinctively yearn for the delights of the circus shows clearly what is missing: the development of the imagination through activities pursued for delight rather than usefulness. Dickens means us to see that the subsequent mistakes and misfortunes of Louisa and Tom are directly attributable to the education they have received, which has starved one side of their natures while concentrating on the other. The inference is that a wise system of education needs to keep the intellectual and the imaginative elements in balance.

3.1(e) Bitzer

Bitzer and Sissy Jupe (see below) form a quartet with Tom and Louisa Gradgrind: although Bitzer and Sissy belong to a lower social class, they too have been subjected to the Gradgrind system and thus enable Dickens to trace the effects of what amounts to an experiment in education. However, the four children are far from being carbon copies of each other: their respective lines of development show that human individuality can produce very different results from like causes. Just as Tom ultimately differs from Louisa (he becomes guilty of a crime as well as morally despicable, whereas she, though tempted, refuses to elope with Harthouse and shows greater humanity than her brother in her dealings with Stephen Blackpool), there is a very marked contrast between Bitzer and Sissy.

When Bitzer is introduced in I,2, he is depicted as physically unattractive and even unwholesome, with his 'cold' eyes and his lack of natural colouring. This coldness and pallor are the external symbols of a moral deficiency, for Bitzer is without feeling for others or indeed any spontaneous impulse at all: his self-centred ambition is the result of the Gradgrind system, which has inculcated a ruthless materialism and calculation of advantages. Bitzer's readiness with the 'definition of a horse' reveals him as a model pupil – an example of the best that the system can produce. His subsequent behaviour, therefore, becomes an unsparing indictment of that system.

The unattractive boy becomes an unattractive young man, ready to spy on his fellow-employees at Bounderby's bank, including Tom. The climax of Bitzer's role in the novel occurs in III,8. At the end of the previous chapter, he has turned up unexpectedly at the circus where Tom is in hiding, and has seized Tom with the intention of handing him over to justice. His motive, needless to say, is not a love of justice for its own sake, but the wish to ingratiate himself with his employer, no doubt blended with malice and envy towards Tom, who has enjoyed advantages in life denied to himself.

In III,8, with masterly irony, Dickens shows Bitzer behaving perfectly consistently while Mr Gradgrind in effect pleads with him to forget all he has been taught. The power of the scene comes from Mr Gradgrind's heart-broken realisation that he himself has produced the situation that now threatens his son: if Bitzer had not been such a prime product of the Gradgrind system, he would not now be responding to Mr Gradgrind's plea, ' "Is [your heart] accessible . . . to any compassionate influence?" ', with the cold but entirely logical reply, ' "It is accessible to Reason, Sir, . . . And to nothing else".' He states that, once he has handed Tom over to Bounderby, he expects to be promoted to Tom's former position in the bank; and when Gradgrind refers to his 'self-interest', he replies:

> 'I am sure you know that the whole social system is a question of self-interest. What you must always appeal to, is a person's self-interest. . . . I was brought up in that catechism when I was very young, Sir, as you are aware.'

The last four words of this speech underline Mr Gradgrind's responsibility for the danger that now threatens Tom.

Bitzer proves impervious to all appeals to his feelings, for he has no feelings. When Gradgrind appeals to his sense of gratitude for the schooling he has received, his reply, though heartless, is in accordance with the principles of calculation in which he has been trained: ' "My schooling was paid for; it was a bargain; and when I came away, the bargain ended." ' The narrator comments: 'It was a fundamental principle of the Gradgraind philosophy that everything was to be paid for. . . . Every inch of the existence of mankind, from birth to death, was to be a bargain across a counter.' Thus both dramatic speech and situation and narrative comment drive home the point that what happens in this scene is the logical outcome of what we have been shown in the schoolroom thirty-four chapters earlier. As we shall see in the next section, the means by which Bitzer is outwitted are entirely appropriate in terms of the symbolic contrasts that form such an important pattern in the novel.

3.1(f) Sissy and the circus

In a speech he gave in 1857, Dickens referred to schools in which 'the bright childish imagination is utterly discouraged'. Sissy Jupe's function in *Hard Times* is partly to show that, once allowed to grow and flourish, the 'bright childish imagination' cannot be easily extinguished. She becomes a pupil at the Gradgrind school, but at a relatively advanced age; before she is exposed to its influence, she has spent her formative years in the circus, and not all the heavy weight of the system can eliminate or suppress the love she has for the things of the imagination. Moreover, the fact that she has developed a 'wisdom of the Heart' rather than a 'wisdom of the Head' makes her much sounder in her moral instincts and moral judgements, and throughout the novel she functions as a touchstone of true wisdom.

The situation is replete with irony, however, for by the standards of the school Sissy is assuredly a failure. She is unable to define a horse in I,2 - though of course she knows far more about horses than anyone else present, and her failure is therefore a reflection on the unsoundness of the educational method rather than on her own shortcomings. In a powerful dialogue with Louisa in I,9, she recounts her further failure to come up to M'Choakumchild's standards: she refers to National Prosperity as Natural Prosperity, and confuses statistics with stutterings (though perhaps Dickens means us to sense a kind of instinctive wisdom even in her errors). She has 'a very dense head for figures', and is rebuked for invoking Christian principles in a discussion of Political Economy. And yet her understanding of the realities behind the arithmetical problems shows that Sissy, the dunce of the school, possesses a wisdom far exceeding that of her teachers: when she is asked to calculate the percentage of those who lose their lives at sea, she replies that a mere statistic is ' "Nothing . . . to the relations and friends of the people that were killed" ' - of no importance, that is to say, compared with the individual human tragedy of their loss.

Why did Dickens decide to make Sissy a child of the circus? It was obviously necessary for Sissy to come from an environment as different as possible from Coketown, the school and the Gradgrind household, into which she is subsequently transferred. The travelling circus, which serves no 'useful' purpose whatsoever but exists solely in order to give pleasure and to bring colour and romance into lives that may otherwise be drab, is a striking antithesis to the world of Coketown. The circus animals, who are often referred to and who play an important part in the outwitting of Bitzer, represent instinct – the opposite of that conscious calculation which is advocated by the Gradgrind philosophy. The drink-sodden but eloquent spokesman for the circus and its values is Mr Sleary, and the reference at the end of I,6 to 'the Sleary philosophy' is intended to form a contrast with 'the Gradgrind philosophy'. In the course of that chapter, Sleary good-humouredly lectures Gradgrind, and the thrust of his remarks is in precisely the opposite direction to the principles and values that we have already come to associate with Gradgrind:

> 'People mutht be amuthed, Thquire, thomehow, . . . they can't be alwayth a working, nor yet they can't be alwayth a learning.'

This scene is balanced and complemented by III,8, in which Sleary is able to render Gradgrind a service in assisting Tom's escape. By a neat symbolic touch, the world of the circus has shown itself to be vitally necessary to the world of Gradgrind, and Bitzer's schemes are outwitted by his moral opposite, Sleary.

Sissy's wisdom and strong moral sense are also shown in her relationship with Louisa. In moral terms, the social difference between Louisa and Sissy is reversed: the circus child who has been given a home out of pity shows herself to be, in all the respects that matter, the superior of the middle-class girl. Sissy is the first to perceive that Louisa's agreement to marry Bounderby is ill advised and bodes disaster; it is she to whom Louisa eventually turns for advice and comfort; and it is she who, by an even bolder reversal of the social roles than that already noted, puts James Harthouse firmly in his place and sends him packing.

Sissy's role in the novel is thus a very important one. Although the 'wisdom of the Head' is embodied in several characters, for much of the action she alone represents the 'wisdom of the Heart'. Its eventual triumph, whereby even Mr Gradgrind acknowledges that Sissy is right, embodies a bold paradox; for Sissy, who, at the beginning of the novel, had seemed to possess less force and power than almost anyone else except Mrs Gradgrind, turns out to be the strongest and most effective of all.

Dickens's presentation of Sissy, and his contrasting of the circus and the school, can be related to a strong tradition that has its origins in the early stages of the Romantic movement, around 1800. The idealisation of the child, whom William Wordsworth refers to in his 'Immortality' ode as a 'mighty prophet', can be traced back to the late-eighteenth-century thinker Jean-Jacques Rousseau, whose immensely influential doctrines represented a reaction against eighteenth-century rationalism. In England, Wordsworth is the first major writer whose work insists on the importance of the instincts and natural impulses as opposed to logic and book-learning; and his influence on subsequent thinkers, poets and novelists is of great significance. His poems urge a 'wise passiveness' and 'spontaneous wisdom', and deplore the effects of detached intellectual enquiry:

> ... Our meddling intellect
> Mis-shapes the beauteous forms of things:
> – We murder to dissect. ('The Tables Turned')

Dickens's attack on the Gradgrind system, and his use of Sissy and the circus to represent 'spontaneous wisdom' and uncalculating goodness of heart, are very much in line with the thinking of Wordsworth, who died only four years before *Hard Times* was written.

Just how wise Sissy's instincts were, without the benefit (or disadvantage) of learning, can be shown by comparing her position with that taken up by a modern historian. Discussing changes in the standard of living in Britain in the first half of the nineteenth century, E. J. Hobsbawm writes in his *Labouring Men* (1964):

> there is no reason why living standards should improve at all times. Whether they do, depends on the distribution of the additional resources produced among the population. But we know that under early industrialism . . . there was no effective mechanism for making the distribution of the national income more equal and several for making it less so. . . .

This is exactly Sissy's point in her comments on what she calls, with touching naïvety, 'Natural Prosperity' (I,9): when M'Choakumchild tells her that there are 'fifty millions of money' in the country, and demands, ' "Isn't this a prosperous nation?" ', she replies, with a perspicacity denied to her teacher, that she cannot answer the question ' "unless I knew who had got the money, and whether any of it was mine" '. Sissy's wise observations on economic inequalities lead us to a consideration of industrialism and the factory system, which produced the wealth that was so unequally distributed.

3.2 INDUSTRIALISM: MASTERS AND WORKERS

During the 1840s – the decade preceding the appearance of *Hard Times* – there emerged a kind of fiction dealing directly and seriously with social problems and with what came to be called the 'condition-of-England question'. Some still-remembered examples are Disraeli's *Sybil* (1845), which gave currency to the idea of the 'two nations' within England, the rich and the poor; and two widely read novels by the Christian Socialist Charles Kingsley, *Yeast* (serialised in 1848) and *Alton Locke* (1850), which drew attention to the sufferings of the poor. A sub-category of this variety of fiction was the so-called 'industrial novel', dealing with life in the teeming new cities. A well-known example, which Dickens admired, was Mrs Elizabeth Gaskell's *Mary Barton* (1848), subtitled 'A Tale of Manchester Life'. Soon after the serialisation of *Hard Times* was completed in *Household Words*, it was followed by another novel about the north of England, Mrs Gaskell's *North and South*.

Hard Times is sometimes treated as an example of the 'industrial novel', but this is a little misleading, since the main action of the novel is (as the earlier part of this chapter has suggested) concerned with a different theme. At the same time the two themes are not, as we shall see, entirely unrelated. This section considers the industrial element and the setting, characters and topics that belong to it.

3.2(a) Coketown

Coketown is intended to be a typical, fairly large industrial town in the north of England. We know that Dickens visited Preston in Lancashire at about the time he began work on *Hard Times*, and there is other evidence (e.g. Stephen Blackpool's surname) that he may have had Lancashire and its cotton towns in mind. But it would be a mistake to attempt to identify Coketown with Preston or any other actual place, even though attempts have sometimes been made to do so (in a letter of 4 September 1866, Dickens states that 'every cotton-spinning town said it was the other cotton-spinning town'). Unlike Mrs Gaskell, who lived in Manchester and knew the life of the poor from first-hand experience, Dickens's experience of the industrial north was limited to short visits. His portrait of Coketown is, as a result, not a detailed account of an actual community based on first-hand experience but a generalised rendering of what might be called the typical or stereotypical northern town.

His account of Coketown, notably in the fifth chapter of the novel, stresses its ugliness and monotony – qualities that are external manifestations of the life and work of its inhabitants. Instead of growing slowly and naturally in response to human needs, such towns have mushroomed as a result of the Industrial Revolution: what had originally been small market-towns became within a few years crowded cities. This growth was solely caused by the profit motive: capitalists built factories and surrounded them with narrow streets of cramped, insanitary houses to accommodate the workers. The 1850s was a period of agitation for sanitary reform, though the great series of public health acts which ensured better standards for such housing came only much later, indeed after Dickens's death. At the time of which he writes, the expectation of life for the inhabitants of these communities was low, partly as a result of the lack of proper diet, insanitary conditions and long hours of work. Sunshine rarely penetrated the pall of smoke that hung over Coketown and its neighbours. (In Manchester at this time the infant mortality rate was 60 per cent.) Dickens tells us that Stephen Blackpool looks older than his years; he is also 'a rather stooping man' (I,10), no doubt as a result of the very long hours spent bending over his machine. Although there had been a series of Factory Acts in the 1830s and 1840s, conditions in the factories – for men, women and children – were still very harsh by modern standards, not only in terms of long hours and infrequent holidays, but owing to the absence of safety regulations (see Section 3.2(e) below).

3.2(b) Stephen Blackpool

As indicated above, Stephen is typical of his class – the skilled but badly paid factory operative – in his poor physical condition and his premature ageing. Stephen, however, is not only a victim of the factory system but has domestic problems that complicate and embitter his life. He is therefore not necessarily representative of the class to which he belongs: in his wish to make Stephen a more dramatically interesting character, Dickens has made him untypical. As it turns out, we see almost nothing of Stephen in his capacity as a worker: we see him leaving the factory, calling on Bounderby, at home in his lodgings, and so forth, but we are given no detailed account of how his time in the factory is actually spent, presumably because Dickens knew little about the subject.

Dickens's critics have generally judged Stephen Blackpool to be a failure on the grounds that, so far from being an acceptable portrayal of a typical factory-worker of the period, he is exceptional, idealised and sentimentalised – a working-class hero rather than a convincing figure. John Ruskin (see p. 75) described him as 'a dramatic perfection, instead of a characteristic example of an honest workman', and this neat formulation has been followed by later critics. George Gissing, writing in 1898 (and himself the author of novels depicting realistically the life of the poorer classes), puts his finger on a serious defect in Dickens's presentation of Stephen when he states that 'Stephen Blackpool represents nothing at all; he is a mere model of meekness, and his great misfortune is such as might befall any man anywhere, the curse of a drunken wife.' Nearer our own time, F. R. Leavis (see p. 77) has said that Stephen is 'too good and qualifies too consistently for the martyr's halo'. It might even be suggested that this character's name reveals Dickens's divided purpose: his surname suggests his Lancashire origins – as does his dialect, on which Dickens evidently expended considerable pains – and seems to promise a realistic treatment; but his Christian name, that of the first Christian martyr (see Acts vi), hints at a more heroic and idealised conception.

At the same time it is not quite fair to say, as Gissing does, that 'the curse of a drunken wife' is Stephen's 'great misfortune' and that this hardly distinguishes him from very different characters in very different novels: it is in fact only *one* of his 'great misfortunes', and we must now look at the tragedy of his position between a hostile employer and hostile fellow-workers.

3.2(c) Bounderby

Bounderby is one of the most important links between the two main themes of the novel, the educational and the industrial. He is a friend of Gradgrind and becomes the husband of Louisa and the employer of Tom; at the same time he is a prominent man of business, 'banker, merchant, manufacturer, and what not' (I,4), and is the owner of the factory at which Stephen and Rachael are employed. For Dickens he represents both a satire on the self-made man whose ruthless methods have enabled him to prosper, and an attack on the heartlessness of the factory-owners; and in the latter capacity Bounderby's qualities emerge most clearly in his relationship with Stephen Blackpool and, specifically, in his two interviews with Stephen in I,11 and II,5.

In the first of these scenes, Bounderby accepts and even glories in the class divisions that separate man from man. When he tells Stephen that there can be no question of his divorcing his wife, since divorce is a luxury available only to the rich, Stephen replies, ' "'Tis just a muddle a'together" ', whereupon Bounderby retorts:

> 'Don't you talk nonsense, my good fellow, . . . about things you don't understand, and don't you call the institutions of your country a muddle, or you'll get yourself into a real muddle one of these fine mornings. The institutions of your country are not your piece-work, and the only thing you have got to do, is, to mind your piece-work. . . . '

The repeated reference to 'the institutions of your country' shows Bounderby's complacent Toryism: it does not occur to him that in some areas, including the law relating to divorce, reform is long overdue, and indeed the word 'reform' is likely to convey to his mind associations with riot and revolution. In the years after the French Revolution (1789) the governing classes in England were much preoccupied with the fear that England might follow suit; and the threat to vested interests represented by the Chartist movement, which arose in the 1830s and demanded a more democratic society, came to a head with a mass meeting and petition to Parliament in 1848 – the 'year of revolutions' in Europe, and only six years before the appearance of *Hard Times*.

In II,5 Bounderby refers to the factory-workers who are trying to form a trade union as 'a set of rascals and rebels whom transportation is too good for': since transportation had been superseded by penal servitude as a form of punishment in 1853, the year before *Hard Times*, this is a neat instance of Bounderby's dogmatic conservatism and refusal to keep up with the times. He also refers to Stephen as 'a tidy specimen' of the kind of trouble-maker to be found among the operatives – ironically enough, since Stephen in fact only wishes for peace and quiet and has refused to join the union because he wants to keep out of trouble and disputes.

Just as Stephen represents an idealised rather than an accurate portrayal of a member of the working classes, Bounderby represents the worst that can be said of the employers at this time. No doubt there were masters who were less ruthless and indifferent, but it suits Dickens's dramatic purposes to make him 'a dramatic monster' – the phrase is Ruskin's and complements his description (quoted above) of Stephen as 'a dramatic perfection'. At the same time the heartlessness of many of the factory-owners, and the subservience of all humane considerations to the profit motive, are a matter of history and could hardly be exaggerated. Nor is Bounderby's entrenched conservatism difficult to parallel from historical examples.

3.2(d) Slackbridge

We saw above that one of the objections that has been raised against Dickens's portrayal of Stephen Blackpool is that he is not a representative of the class to which he belongs but a man with exceptional problems, not all of which are directly related to his role as a factory-hand. Objections have also been made to the characterisation of Slackbridge, the agitator; and in this case there is a curious inconsistency between what Dickens offers in the novel and what he had done a little earlier in the *Household Words* article 'On Strike' (see p. 6), which records his very recent impressions of the situation in Preston.

Strikes were not at all uncommon in England in the early 1850s – there had, for instance, been a much-publicised strike of the Amalgamated Society of Engineers in Manchester in 1851 – but the strike of the Preston weavers attracted a great deal of attention, partly on account of its scale (over 20,000 workers were involved), and partly because it lasted for twenty-nine weeks and for most of that time the outcome seemed uncertain. Starting as a strike for a 10 per cent increase in wages, it turned into a lock-out when the owners closed the mills and hoped to starve the workers into submission (hitherto those on strike had been maintained by donations from those who were still working). It thus turned into a full-scale confrontation between capital and labour; and soon other communities were involved, since the Preston workers could only continue to strike with the support of contributions from workers in neighbouring towns.

As Geoffrey Carnall notes in his essay 'Dickens, Mrs Gaskell, and the Preston Strike' (*Victorian Studies*, 1964), the eyes of England were turned upon Preston: '*The Times* and *Daily News* sent special correspondents. The *Illustrated London News* sent an artist. The strike was the subject of leading articles, magazine features, and innumerable letters-to-the-editor.' Dickens had two reasons for going to Preston: not only was he anxious to collect material for his new novel, but he wanted to write something that would show that his magazine *Household Words* was abreast of contemporary issues. While in Preston he attended a meeting of factory-workers and listened to the orators who addressed them. One of them was a certain Mortimer Grimshaw, who appears in the article thinly disguised as 'Gruffshaw' and was probably the prototype for Slackbridge.

Grimshaw, like Slackbridge, seems to have been a mob orator with an abrasive style: another journalist who heard him described him as speaking 'with a dogmatical invective and a blatant vituperation more worthy of a Russian despot than an English patriot'. But – and this is the really significant point – Grimshaw was not the leader of the Preston weavers: this was George Cowell, who seems to have been a man of much more moderate views and who was a local man, not an agitator brought in from outside like Slackbridge. There is thus a distinct element of unfairness in Dickens's use of Slackbridge as a typical union leader: in depicting him as he does, Dickens is loading the dice against the unions and shows a marked hostility towards their activities. On similar and complementary lines, it might also be maintained that the use of Bounderby as a typical boss is not much less unfair. But Dickens's art, like that of fairy-tale and melodrama, relies heavily on conventions to which realistic notions of 'fairness' are largely irrelevant: he characteristically presents an extreme case in order to make his point as emphatically as possible.

As Carnall says, 'there is a notable discrepancy between the portrait of trade-unionism in the Preston article and in the novel'. Why should Dickens have changed his attitude in such a short time? The answer must be, I think, not in terms of Dickens's politics but in terms of the difference between a piece of reporting and a work of fiction: in the latter, Slackbridge's demagogic methods, and his success in leading the miners to send Stephen to Coventry against their natural instincts and better judgement, create a more dramatic situation both in the short and in the long term. In the short term Slackbridge's oratorical style and ruthless attitudes (no less ruthless than Bounderby's, though quite different in their origins) produce a more powerful scene than the more moderate stance of a man such as Cowell would have done; and in the long term his fellow-workers' lack of support adds considerably to Stephen's burden and causes him to be sacked by Bounderby and hence to leave Coketown.

In the process, however, Dickens has sacrificed realism and authenticity in his portrayal of Slackbridge; and many of his critics have viewed this character as an inaccurate and unfair presentation of the prevailing mood of the trades unions at the time. G. B. Shaw (see p. 76), for instance, sees him as 'a mere figment of the middle-class imagination', and adds: 'No such man would be listened to by a meeting of

English factory hands.' Edgar Johnson echoes Shaw in calling Slackbridge 'a figment of [Dickens's] imagination'; and F. R. Leavis sums up this element as a weakness in a great novel:

> when Dickens comes to the Trade Unions his understanding of the world he offers to deal with betrays a marked limitation. There were undoubtedly professional agitators, and Trade Union solidarity was undoubtedly often asserted at the expense of the individual's rights, but it is a score against a work so insistently typical in intention that it should give the representative role to the agitator, Slackbridge, and make Trade Unionism nothing better than the pardonable error of the misguided and oppressed, and, as such, an agent in the martyrdom of the good working man.

3.2(e) Factory accidents

One of the features of the early stages of the Industrial Revolution was the appalling hazards faced by the workers, ranging from unguarded machines in factories to explosions in coal-mines. Dickens touches on this in *Hard Times* in III,6. Not only is the manner of Stephen's death – a disused mine-shaft that has been left as a menace to the unwary passer-by – directly related to the negligence and indifference of the masters who were unwilling to spend a small fraction of their profits on safeguarding their workers; but Stephen includes a direct reference to the topic in his dying speech, where he says that, while still being worked, the pit cost 'hundreds and hundreds o' men's lives', and is still claiming lives even after it is worked no longer: ' "When it were in work, it killed wi'out need; when 'tis let alone, it kills wi'out need." ' For Dickens, and for the reader, the disused mine-shaft is not only a highly specific problem, which appropriate legislation could deal with (as it eventually did) if public indifference turned to concern, but a powerful emblem of man's inhumanity to man.

3.3 MARRIAGE AND DIVORCE

In *Hard Times* two marriages are of particular importance – the short-lived one between Louisa and Bounderby, and the one of much longer standing between Stephen and his drunken wife – and they both come to grief. It may be significant that, by the time he wrote the novel,

Dickens's own marriage, which was eighteen years old (almost exactly the same as Stephen's), was beginning to run into difficulties; and only four years after the novel appeared he and his wife obtained a legal separation. Apart from any personal element, however, the subject was a highly topical one; for it had been widely discussed in the previous year (1853), and a Royal Commission had recommended that petitions for divorce should be dealt with by civil rather than ecclesiastical courts. In June 1854, while the serialisation of *Hard Times* was still in progress, the House of Lords had debated the subject but rejected a bill to amend the law.

It was only in 1857, three years after the novel was published, that a law was passed establishing a new court (the Divorce and Matrimonial Causes Court) and thereby simplifying the hitherto cumbrous and expensive process of obtaining a divorce. Further legislation followed later in the nineteenth century, and the numbers of those obtaining divorces speak for themselves. Between the sixteenth century and 1857 (i.e. until the new law was passed), there had been only 317 divorces in England – a startlingly low figure until we recall that an act of parliament was required in each instance. In 1858 there were 200 divorces; but forty years later, in 1898, the number had risen to over 5000.

It is in this context that we must read the scene between Stephen and Bounderby in I,11. As David Craig has said, Stephen's statement of his case and the argument that follows are 'a good example of Dickens's humane propaganda on the most vexing and topical kinds of social issue'. Towards the end of the chapter, Bounderby tells Stephen what process he will have to go through in order to divorce the woman who has ceased to be a wife in anything except name:

> 'Why, you'd have to go to Doctors' Commons with a suit, and you'd have to go to the House of Lords with a suit, and you'd have to get an Act of Parliament to enable you to marry again, and it would cost you (if it was a case of very plain sailing), I suppose from a thousand to fifteen hundred pound. . . . Perhaps twice the money.'

(Doctors' Commons was an ecclesiastical court, in which Dickens had briefly worked in his youth as a shorthand-writer.) Such a process was obviously far beyond the means of a man like Stephen, or indeed for any except the rich, since we probably need to multiply the sum by at least ten or twenty times to obtain a sense of its size in present-day values.

Bounderby's unsympathetic enumeration of the necessary steps constitutes a satire on Dickens's part on the archaic and clumsy machinery of the law. It has been suggested that Dickens may have had in mind some comments made by a judge, Lord Justice Maule, in 1845. Showing an obvious sympathy with a man who was technically guilty of bigamy, Maule described what the unfortunate man should have done – the process described also by Bounderby – and concluded: 'It is quite true that these proceedings would have cost you many hundreds of pounds, whereas you probably have not as many pence', adding ironically: 'But the law knows no distinction between rich and poor.' This flagrant distinction is Dickens's theme in the scene between Stephen and Bounderby.

Bounderby's remarks to Stephen on the 'sanctity' of marriage and the need to preserve the 'institutions' of the country have a very hollow ring in the face of the grim reality of Stephen's marriage; and their hypocrisy becomes evident when he refuses to have his own wife back in his home after she has left him. Since Bounderby was a rich man, he would, of course, had had little difficulty in obtaining a divorce had there been adequate grounds for doing so – for instance, if Louisa had actually committed adultery with Harthouse.

4 TECHNICAL FEATURES

4.1 PLOT AND STRUCTURE

Hard Times acquires its distinctive shape or form from at least three different elements that may be described as structural principles. The first is that of plot: the arrangement of actions in a way that reflects cause and effect as well as chronology. Thus Louisa's marriage leads to her cold treatment of her husband and eventually their separation; Tom's gambling leads to crime, detection and punishment. On another level, the novel is structured by the ideas for which it is a vehicle: the antithesis between 'fact' and 'fancy', the school and the circus, calculation and instinct, self-seeking and compassion, belongs to the realm of moral and ethical ideas, though – since this is a novel and not a treatise – it is constantly presented in concrete and dramatic form, through contrasts of setting, character, behaviour and speech. Thirdly, there is a less obvious but powerful principle of structure that is associated more readily with poetry and poetic drama, such as Shakespearean tragedy, than with fiction, but which Dickens was by this stage in his career using with great skill and to great effect. This is the deployment of images and symbols, some of them recurring throughout the book and therefore helping to give it unity. In this section we shall be mainly concerned with the first of these elements, that of 'plot'. The second has been examined in the previous chapter, and the third is discussed in Section 4.4, below.

As the author of a novel intended or serialisation, Dickens needed a strong plot to stimulate the reader's curiosity and keep him reading (and buying the magazine) from week to week. Most Victorian novels are fairly heavily plotted, the relatively plotless novels of modern times only emerging after serialisation had ceased to be an important means of presenting fiction to the public. But there is no doubt that a plot also made a strong appeal to Dickens's tastes and temperament: it enabled him to trace the way in which later events proceeded from definable causes, and – since the novelist plays the role of God in the world created by his own novel – to perform a providential role in the distribution of rewards and punishments.

The plot and sub-plot of *Hard Times* have already been distinguished (see p. 36), and the point has also been made that Dickens carefully establishes many connexions between the two, so that they do not exist independently and threaten to break the novel into two, but constantly touch and intersect. The further point may be made that the plot accommodates an abundance of 'plotting' in another sense of the word: Harthouse plots to seduce Louisa, Mrs Sparsit plots to betray them both, Tom plots to make Stephen appear to be a criminal, Bitzer plots to bring Tom to justice, Slearly plots to outwit Bitzer, and so forth. As well as plots there are mysteries: for example, who is Mrs Pegler? what has happened to Stephen when he fails to return to Coketown? what has become of Sissy's father? These plots and mysteries, again, help to spur on the reader by arousing his curiosity, and thus counteract the flagging of interest that may occur during the months of serialisation.

The plots devised and executed, with different degrees of success, by various characters are the result of human intentions; but there are other aspects of the action that proceed from accident, and some of these must be regarded as examples of Dickens's dependence upon coincidence. In II,6, for instance – an important chapter in its bearing upon later events – it is perhaps a little unlikely that Stephen, Rachael, Mrs Pegler, Louisa and Tom should all happen to come together in the same room at the same time, though such a chance assembly is certainly not impossible and life constantly furnishes coincidences far more striking and improbable. Again, in III,6, it is a very lucky chance that makes Rachael and Sissy take a country walk on a certain day in a certain direction, and thus stumble upon evidence of Stephen's whereabouts just in time to hear his dying words. This obviously makes a far more effective narrative than if, for instance, they had come across his dead body, or someone else had found him, or he had been found long afterwards: but when we stop to think about the scene we are likely to conclude that there is some forcing of probability. However, it is a tribute to the skill of Dickens's narrative that, when actually in the process of reading, we are very unlikely to be troubled by such considerations.

The further point has sometimes been made that, in the context of Christian beliefs, what may superficially appear to be accident or coincidence is really divinely ordered; and, to return to our last example, Rachael and Sissy are led by Heaven to find Stephen. Though alien to many modern readers, such a conviction would not have seemed at all strange to many of Dickens's readers, or indeed to Dickens himself.

The ending of the novel provides a good example of the novelist playing the role of Providence: not only are all the loose ends of the plot neatly tied up, but the various major characters receive punishment (e.g. Bounderby, Tom) or reward (e.g. Sissy) according to their deserts; and the novel concludes with a glance at their subsequent lives, beyond the compass of the novel's central action.

One further aspect of the structure of *Hard Times* remains to be noted. The final version of the novel is divided into 'Books' as well as chapters, and each 'Book' and chapter has its own title. This inevitably contributes to the reader's experience, since the beginning or ending of a chapter, and still more of a 'Book', derives a special prominence from its position. The three 'Books' give the novel a structure not unlike that of a three-act play. The first ends with Louisa's marriage to Bounderby – an event that leads naturally into the second part of the novel, since we are bound to wonder how such an ill-omened marriage will turn out. The second ends with Louisa's return home after the collapse of her marriage: as she lies unconscious at her father's feet, we almost seem to see the curtain descending. The third part of the novel, like the final act of a drama, is concerned with solving outstanding mysteries (including the bank robbery and the identity of Mrs Pegler) and bringing the story to a conclusion.

4.2 CHARACTERISATION

Dickens took considerable pains over naming his characters, and the blend of realism and symbolism that is often to be found in his names is typical of the dual nature of his art. A name such as that of Stephen Blackpool, for instance, seems at first sight to be authentic and unremarkable; but it represents (as already suggested in 3.2(b)) two major aspects of Stephen's character – that he is a northerner and that he suffers and dies after being subjected to a kind of martyrdom. Some of the other names are less susceptible to a ready explanation, but are at the same time undeniably suggestive: Sparsit suggests sparse, and perhaps Sleary is related to slurred and Harthouse to heartless. Gradgrind suggests not only the mills of Coketown, but the remorseless grinding away at 'hard facts', as well as, possibly, a reference to the political theorist James Mill (see p. 38). Bounderby is certainly a bounder in the once common sense of 'a vulgarly irrepressible man' (Eric Partridge's *Dictionary of Slang and Unconventional English*) Perhaps the most outrageously improbable name in the book is that of M'Choakumchild, for it seems altogether too neatly appropriate for a schoolmaster who stuffs his pupils with facts (for its probable reference to the educationist M'Culloch see p. 40).

Such an audacious blending of the probable and the incredible, the realistic and the symbolic or highly stylised, is to be found not only in Dickens's names but in his methods of characterisation. A character such as Bounderby, for instance, is shown to have a particular role in society and to be involved in specific social and personal relationships: so much for the realistic element in his presentation. But his speech and behaviour throughout the book are exaggerated to the point of carica-ture: the world is full of bullies and boasters, but we cannot believe that any of them would talk or act as Bounderby does.

We are alerted to this non-realistic element when Bounderby first appears (I,4). Dickens's description is rich in figurative language ('a metallic laugh', 'inflated like a balloon', 'that brassy speaking-trumpet of a voice of his'): this is not an account of a man that tries to persuade us of its truth to nature, but a highly stylised portrait in which one or two leading characteristics are highlighted and everything else is omitted. Such a character is easy to visualise and easy to remember, and this was an important consideration in the circumstances of serialisation. Just as the eccentric names already referred to would be readily recognised when the character reappeared, the characters drawn with a few bold strokes would make a strong and definite impression on the reader and would not be confused with other characters.

Although Bounderby perhaps shows Dickens's tendency to exag-geration and caricature at its most extreme, several other characters are presented in similar terms. On the very first page of the novel, for instance, the description of Mr Gradgrind is not only strongly *visual* but is highly *symbolic* – that is, the external qualities referred to are seen, sooner or later, to correspond to qualities of mind or character. Gradgrind has a 'square forefinger', a 'square wall of a forehead', 'square legs, square shoulders', a 'square coat' and a mouth that is 'wide, thin, and hard set'. All of this signals Mr Gradgrind's rigid, inflexible nature. As with the description of Bounderby, the use of language and imagery may be described as poetic. Mr Gradgrind's eyes 'found commodious cellarage in two dark caves', and his bald head was 'covered with knobs, like the crust of a plum pie, as if the head had scarcely warehouse-room for the hard facts stored inside'. Such statements work not only directly but, like poetry, obliquely, through suggestion and allusion: the estate agent's language ('commodious cellarage') and the reference to the world of commerce ('warehouse-room') ensure that we not only have a sense of what the character looks like but begin to understand the values of the world he inhabits and the motives that impel him.

Poetic imagery is again to be found in I,2 where Sissy and Bitzer are introduced. The 'lustrous colour' of Sissy, with her dark eyes and dark hair, contrasts boldly with the pallid and 'short-cropped' Bitzer: already the reader perceives that these two children represent not only different physical types but opposite sets of qualities. In all these examples, *external* qualities are to be interpreted as signs of *internal* attributes. Dickens sometimes goes even further than this, and makes objects act as extensions of their owner's personality or reflections of his nature. Thus the account of Mr Gradgrind's house, Stone Lodge, in I,3 explicitly looks back to the earlier description of its owner: 'A great square house, with a heavy portico darkening the principal windows, as its master's heavy brows overshadowed his eyes.' By a transformation like that in a fairy-tale or a dream, Dickens seems almost to have turned Mr Gradgrind into a building; and this quality of 'animism' (the description of objects as if they were living creatures) is very characteristic of Dickens.

One corollary of all this is that we see very little of the inner life of Dickens's characters. Whereas some novelists take pains to give the reader an insight into a character's secret life and unspoken thoughts, Dickens works for the most part through a brilliant and memorable depiction of externals. We see and hear a good deal of, for instance, Mr Bounderby, but we have little sense of what is passing in his mind or what he thinks about when he is alone. Dickens's method, that is, is to a great extent *dramatic* – and this is a point we shall now explore a little further.

4.3 STYLE AND LANGUAGE

As already mentioned in Chapter 1, Dickens as a young man had a passionate interest in the stage: he thought seriously of becoming an actor, and retained this enthusiasm throughout his life. Evidence of his interest in the drama can be seen in his novels. His presentation of character, for instance, is largely through action and speech; and this is precisely what we find in the theatre, where analysis and comment is difficult if not impossible to convey. A comparison has already been made between the three Books of *Hard Times* and a three-act drama (see Section 4.1, above); and this comparison can be pursued in more detail. Dickens presents his story through a series of 'scenes' that simultaneously develop the action and the charaters and embody the themes of the novel. We begin with a scene in the schoolroom; pass on to a scene outside the circus; and continue through a large number of scenes of major or minor importance. The 'big scenes' such as the two interviews between Louisa and her father, or the one in which Mrs Sparsit spies on Louisa and Harthouse, have a strong theatrical quality; and it is no surprise that Dickens's novels were very popular in stage versions during his lifetime and in our own time have been successful in the cinema and on television.

The most obviously dramatic element in a novel is the dialogue, in which the characters seem to 'speak' to the reader as the actors in a play speak to the audience. Dialogue is particularly important in Dickens's novels, and in many of his chapters it carries a heavier burden of significance than any other element such as narrative, description or comment. A notable feature of his dialogue is the contrasts of style to be found in the speech assigned to different characters: we may say that the characters are *individualised* through their speech, as well as – and usually somewhat more than – through the way in which they are described. After an initial passage of description when the character appears for the first time, Dickens normally relies on dialogue to maintain and extend the character's individuality; and it is hardly an exaggeration to say that no two characters talk in exactly the same way. Even Louisa and Tom, who belong to the same family, are carefully differentiated.

Some of these differentiations are very obvious, and, like the other boldly drawn aspects of character referred to in Section 4.2, they assist the reader in recognising a character when it reappears. There are, for example, long stretches of the novel in which Mr Sleary does not appear, but his lisping pronunciation makes him easy to identify even if we have not encountered him for days or weeks of reading.

The dialogue given to Stephen Blackpool would probably not strike an expert on the Lancashire dialect as very authentic, and it was in fact a form of regional speech of which Dickens knew almost nothing (unlike Cockney, which he had known from childhood and uses much more extensively in his novels). But what is important is that it does serve to individualise Stephen – and after all few readers, then or now, are in a position to judge its accuracy. The point about Stephen's dialect is that it contrasts him with other characters: in the scenes with Bounderby, for instance, it is one of the elements that marks the social and economic gap between them.

Dickens sometimes went to considerable pains to ensure the authenticity of his characters' speech. On 20 February 1854, for instance, not long after he had begun the novel and possibly when he was preparing to write I,6, in which the circus folk appear and talk at some length, he wrote to his friend Mark Lemon:

> Will you note down and send me any slang terms among the tumblers and circus-people that you can call to mind? I have noted down some – I want them in my new story. . . .

This suggests that, for all its frequent exaggeration and stylisation, Dickens's dialogue can also be accurate and authentic.

Though very important, dialogue is of course only one of the elements in a Dickens novel; and something needs to be said about the use of language in the non-dialogue passages. For a substantial part of the text, the 'voice' that speaks to us may be loosely regarded as that of Dickens, but ought more properly to be referred to as that of the narrator. This 'voice' has its own distinctive style: clear, confident, argumentative, often ironical or scornful, though sometimes full of compassion.

In an interesting essay, 'The Rhetoric of *Hard Times*', David Lodge suggests that 'rhetoric' – the use of language to persuade, as in a political speech – is an appropriate term to use in connection with Dickens's work. He adds:

> Not only is the 'author's voice' always insistent in his novels, but it is characteristically a public-speaking voice, an oratorical or histrionic voice; and it is not difficult to see a connection be-

tween this feature of his prose and his fondness for speech-making and public reading of his works.

The description of Gradgrind's house in I,3, already referred to, is a good example of this rhetoric. The style of the passage has the same emphatic, dogmatic quality that belongs both to Gradgrind's speech and to his philosophy: 'Six windows on this side of the door, six on that side. . .' – such statements admit no contradiction or argument, any more than Gradgrind will tolerate another point of view. A striking feature of the passage is the fondness for sentences without main verbs ('A great square house . . .'; 'A lawn and garden . . .'; etc.), as if the 'fact' of the house and its various features were being presented to us in its stark simplicity.

A third variety of style is that used in the narrative passages: those describing a sequence of events. They are not very numerous in *Hard Times*, since, as already noted, so much of the business of the novel is conducted through dialogue; but a good example is the passage in III,6 where Sissy runs for help and brings back a rescue party after she and Rachael have discovered the injured Stephen at the bottom of the mine-shaft. Unusually in this novel, for a couple of pages there is not a single line of dialogue; and the excitement and urgency are very well conveyed. Even here, though, it is revealing that we are made aware of the narrator's voice, when it apostrophises (appears to speak directly to) Sissy: 'Run, Sissy, run, in Heaven's name! Don't stop for breath. Run, run!' This is not dialogue in the normal sense, for we are not meant to suppose that the words were ever spoken: rather, it is as if the narrator had for the moment become a bystander watching the drama.

4.4 IMAGE AND SYMBOL

Dickens knew his Shakespeare extremely well, and it may have been from Shakespeare's great tragedies that he learned that unity can be given to a long and complex work by the use of recurring images. In *Hard Times* we find in different parts of the novel, for instance, a number of images related to fire and smoke. The smoke from the chimneys of Coketown – literal and visible smoke that is a sign of the intense fires needed to provide power for the steam-driven engines – is prominent in the description of the town at the beginning of I,5. In I,8 there is a whole sequence of references to fire: Louisa and Tom sit by the fireside of their home, Louisa 'looking at the bright sparks as they dropped upon the hearth'; later she tells Tom she is 'looking at the fire'; and there is a reference to the children's shadows 'defined upon the wall' and overhung by other shadows as if 'by a dark cavern'. It seems clear that this is not just a literal fire but the symbol of something more intangible; and before the end of the chapter Dickens enables us to interpret the symbol.

Louisa stares into the fire so intently that Tom is impelled 'to contemplate the fire which so engrossed her, . . . and see what he could make of it'. He makes nothing of it, finding it 'as stupid and blank as everything else looks' but he asks Louisa what she sees in it ('Not a circus?'). Louisa replies that it has made her think about their future. In this way the contrasting natures of the two are brought out: Louisa is the more sensitive, thoughtful and imaginative (though her imagination has been repressed by her upbringing), her brother moody and indifferent. Looking for 'pictures in the fire' was a traditional method of amusement and even of fortune-telling, and Louisa's anxiety to see what the future holds betrays her anxiety as she moves towards her marriage to Bounderby.

In the same chapter there appears, less prominently, another firemetaphor: speaking bitterly and 'spitefully' about the 'Facts' and 'Figures' that plague his life, Tom says, '. . . I wish I could put a thousand barrels of gunpowder under them, and blow them all up together!' This metaphor reappears in the titles of II,7 and 8 ('Gunpowder' and 'Explosion').

The image of fire is again important in the crucial scene between Louisa and her father in I,15. When Louisa, having been asked whether she will marry Bounderby, looks out of the window, Gradgrind asks her, 'Are you consulting the chimneys of the Coketown works . . .?' to which she replies, 'There seems to be nothing there but languid and monotonous smoke. Yet when the night comes, Fire bursts out, father!' Gradgrind does not 'see the application of the remark'; but the reader, more perceptive, realises that Louisa's own suppressed fires may eventually burst out, as indeed they do; or, more literally, her passionate nature, though restrained and concealed by the upbringing she has received, will assert itself at last, leading to the collapse of her marriage.

Smoke and fire do not provide the only cluster of images in the novel. Consider, for example, the use made of references to flowers and animals, from the flowers on the carpet referred to in the schoolroom scene to the flower that Tom idly pulls to pieces, and from the faithful dog Merrylegs to the circus animals who play a part in Tom's rescue. As these connections with the world of the circus suggest, flowers and animals represent the world of beauty and instinct that is denied by the Gradgrind philosophy, but that after all demonstrates its indispensable role in the fully human experience.

Other examples of image and symbol may be more briefly noted. The Gradgrind home, Stone Lodge, is a very solid symbol of the Gradgrind values and outlook. The mine-shaft down which Stephen falls is not only a physical feature but a symbol of the employers' lack of concern for their workers' safety, as Dickens makes explicit in Stephen's dying speech. And the thunderstorm in II,11 is not just a meteorological phenomenon but an external symbol of the passion and conflict within Louisa, who at this point in the story is torn between the temptation to run away with Harthouse and her sense of right and wrong.

5 A SPECIMEN PASSAGE AND COMMENTARY

No single extract could be fully representative of Dickens's art in *Hard Times*; but the following analysis is offered as an example that may be helpful to the student called upon to undertake a similar exercise. It forms the opening of Book I, Chapter 5 ('The Keynote'), and the lines are numbered here for ease of reference.

COKETOWN, to which Messrs Bounderby and Gradgrind now walked, was a triumph of fact; it had no greater taint of fancy in it than Mrs Gradgrind herself. Let us strike the key-note, Coketown, before pursuing our tune.

5   It was a town of red brick, or of brick that would have been red if the smoke and ashes had allowed it; but, as matters stood it was a town of unnatural red and black like the painted face of a savage. It was a town of machinery and tall chimneys, out of which interminable serpents of smoke trailed themselves for ever
10   and ever, and never got uncoiled. It had a black canal in it, and a river that ran purple with ill-smelling dye, and vast piles of building full of windows where there was a rattling and a trembling all day long, and where the piston of the steam-engine worked monotonously up and down, like the head of an elephant in a
15   state of melancholy madness. It contained several large streets all very like one another, and many small streets still more like one another, inhabited by people equally like one another, who all went in and out at the same hours, with the same sound upon the same pavements, to do the same work, and to whom every day
20   was the same as yesterday and tomorrow, and every year the counterpart of the last and the next.

These attributes of Coketown were in the main inseparable from the work by which it was sustained; against them were to be set off, comforts of life which found their way all over the world,
25 and elegancies of life which made, we will not ask how much of the fine lady, who could scarcely bear to hear the place mentioned. The rest of its features were voluntary, and they were these.

You saw nothing in Coketown but what was severely workful.
30 If the members of a religious persuasion built a chapel there – as the members of eighteen religious persuasions had done – they made it a pious warehouse of red brick, with sometimes (but this only in highly ornamented examples) a bell in a bird-cage on the top of it. The solitary exception was the New Church; a stuccoed
35 edifice with a square steeple over the door, terminating in four short pinnacles like florid wooden legs. All the public inscriptions in the town were painted alike, in severe characters of black and white. The jail might have been the infirmary, the infirmary might have been the jail, the town-hall might have been either, or both,
40 or anything else, for anything that appeared to the contrary in the graces of their construction. Fact, fact, fact, everywhere in the material aspect of the town; fact, fact, fact, everywhere in the immaterial. The M'Choakumchild school was all fact, and the school of design was all fact, and the relations between master
45 and man were all fact, and everything was fact between the lying-in hospital and the cemetery, and what you couldn't state in figures, or show to be purchaseable in the cheapest market and saleable in the dearest, was not, and never should be, world without end, Amen.

In *Hard Times* Dickens's characteristic mode is dramatic: that is, he works through scenes in which the meaning is largely conveyed through action and dialogue. The above passage is, therefore, exceptional in that it consists of a sustained description in which the narrator is addressing the reader directly rather than through the characters of the novel. At the same time its importance is indicated by the chapter-title, echoed in the opening paragraph ('Let us strike the key-note . . .'). In music the key-note is that to which the melody returns, however far it may wander from it; and Dickens challenges the reader to grasp in what sense Coketown is the 'key-note' of the book.

To an extent unusual in Dickens's novels, the action in *Hard Times* is concentrated in a few places; and all these places - among them Gradgrind's house (Stone Lodge), Bounderby's house and his bank, Stephen Blackpool's lodgings and the factory where he works - are in Coketown or in its immediate vicinity. When characters leave Coketown and go elsewhere, as Bounderby, Gradgrind and Mrs Sparsit all go to London, Harthouse goes on a shooting trip to Yorkshire and Stephen seeks work at a distance after he has lost his job, we do not follow them there: the action remains firmly set in Coketown. The name is, of course, fictitious and (like many of Dickens's names) symbolic as well as descriptive: coke is not only associated with industrial processes but is a hard, unyielding, severely practical substance, a physical equivalent of the principles and values that the town represents. There is no need to try to identify Coketown with any actual town or city that Dickens may have visited or heard of: it is a typical large industrial community in the north of England and has no doubt grown very rapidly in the early nineteenth century in response to the spread of the industrial system. (Preston, for instance, which Dickens certainly saw at first-hand, had fewer than 12,000 inhabitants in 1801; fifty years later, shortly before *Hard Times* was written, its population was almost 70,000.)

The short opening paragraph describes Coketown as 'a triumph of fact' - a point to be developed with a wealth of detail in the rest of the passage - and reminds the reader of the antithesis of 'fact' and 'fancy' that has already been established in the opening scene in the school-room and will continue to appear throughout the book. We are told that the 'taint of fancy' has been excluded from the town; but at this point we may recall that the word was first used (in the second chapter) by Sissy Jupe, and we may reflect that, even though Sussy was immediately rebuked by one of the representatives of 'fact' ('you mustn't fancy'), her presence may turn out to be a potent one.

The second paragraph makes two main points: that Coketown is *unnatural* (the word occurs in the first sentence), and that it is *monotonous*. These points are not made abstractly, however, but through graphic detail and poetic imagery. The red-brick buildings made grimy by dense smoke are compared to 'the painted face of a savage' (line 7), and the implication of the simile is that there is something barbarous and potentially destructive about such an environment (located, paradoxically, in the country that considered itself the most advanced in the world). Dickens's imagination develops these details and images rather than giving them to us once and for all, so that the point is pressed home and can hardly be missed by even the most careless or insensitive of his readers – and many of those readers will, of course, belong to the social class of Bounderby and Gradgrind rather than that of Stephen Blackpool. Thus the garish colours of the savage's 'painted face' are reinforced by the 'river that ran purple with ill-smelling dye' (line 11), another instance of the 'unnatural'. (Note, too, that a double appeal is made to the visual sense and the sense of smell.) The associations of 'savage' are also developed with the reference to 'serpents of smoke' (line 9) and the comparison of the steam-engine pistons to the movements of a tormented elephant (line 14). These references to wild animals may be contrasted with the use elsewhere in the novel, of domesticated animals: if Coketown is associated with untamed beasts, the circus that is its symbolic opposite is associated with horses and dogs which exist on good terms with human beings and are capable (like the dog Merrylegs) of showing loyalty and devotion.

The regularity and monotony of the town-planning is the result of a rapid growth that is itself 'unnatural': instead of growing slowly and in response to human needs, the town has mushroomed to satisfy the profit motive, cheap and inadequate housing having been jerry-built to accommodate the army of workers required for the new factories. The long sentence beginning 'It contained several large streets . . .' suggests, through its length and structure, the monotony of the lives of those who dwell in those streets, for Dickens sees the visible aspects of the town as an expression of, or a metaphor for, the dullness of the lives to which the inhabitants are condemned.

The third paragraph forms a bridge between the longer paragraphs that precede and follow it, and places Coketown in the context of the industrial system as a whole. Although Dickens does not actually use the phrase, his comments remind us that Britain at this time was generally regarded as 'the workshop of the world'. The products of Coketown find their way 'all over the world'. So far from unifying the human race, however, this merely stresses the 'two nations' of the haves and the have-nots; for, as Dickens points out, the 'fine lady' who benefits from the labours of the Coketown workers can 'scarcely bear to hear the place mentioned'. Dickens's ironical implication – borne out more fully elsewhere in the novel – is that those who produce the 'comforts of life' have little or no share in the enjoyment of them.

The irony of the third paragraph leads naturally into the satirical observations on organised religion in the fourth, which turns from the work and homes of the Coketown employees to the spiritual provision and social institutions to be found in the town. The north of England has traditionally been a stronghold of nonconformism, and Dickens's reference to the 'eighteen religious persuasions' that have erected chapels hints at the rivalry between different sects and the often minute theological and liturgical differences that separate them. (Dickens's own Christianity was of a much more general, tolerant, non-institutional kind.) The other public buildings (jail, infirmary, town-hall) are indistinguishable from each other: their designs are, as it were, machine-made and mass-produced rather than expressing and accommodating the different functions they are intended to serve; and in this respect they again offer a parallel to the loss of individuality suffered by the Coketown workers, whose appearance and life-styles have had a dull uniformity imposed upon them by the demands of the factory system. The last sentence of the extract explicitly links public buildings such as the school with intangibles such as 'the relations between master and man': the relentless laws of a capitalist economy in which the profit motive is paramount govern the whole of life from birth to death ('the lying-in hospital and the cemetery'). The final words are taken from the Book of Common Prayer but are applied to the 'gospel' of fact and the 'worship' of money: their ironical use thus looks back to the references to the ineffectual presence of organised religion earlier in the paragraph.

A striking feature of Dickens's description in this passage is that he is not *simply* giving us an account of the visible scene, but is using concrete details such as the architectural styles of particular buildings to convey a sense of an economic philosophy and a set of moral or ethical attitudes; so that the passage ranges in its subject-matter and its applications from smoking factory-chimneys to 'the relations between master and man', and from a polluted river to the failure of organised religion to lighten the spiritual darkness of the inhabitants. This bringing together of the concrete and the abstract is summed up in the penultimate sentence of the extract, in which the key-word 'fact' appears six times and is shown to be manifested in both the 'material' and the 'immaterial' aspects of the town.

The repetition of the word 'fact' is only one example of a favourite Dickensian stylistic device that is very much in evidence in this passage.

At its simplest level it is to be found in the reiteration of a single word; but it also appears in the use of recurring sentence-patterns. Thus the four sentences of the second paragraph (lines 5–21) begin, respectively: 'It was a town . . .', 'It was a town . . .', 'It had . . .', 'It contained . . .' Such lack of variety in sentence-openings would usually be regarded as a defect; but Dickens has a definite and twofold purpose. His theme, after all, is monotony; and the repeated pattern imitates or enacts as well as referring to the machine-like principles by which everything in Coketown is regulated, from the architecture to the daily time-tables of the workers. Repetition is also a device for producing emphasis, and the sentences strike the reader's ear and mind with an unmistakable urgency.

The last sentence of the second paragraph (lines 15–21) is another good example of the use of repetition in order to emphasise the crushing monotony of Coketown life. The phrase 'like one another' occurs three times, and the word 'same' five times. Apart from words and phrases, the structure of the sentence embodies a principle of repetition, as can be seen by a little rearrangement of it:

It contained several large streets	/	all very like one another,
and many small streets	/	still more like one another,
inhabited by people	/	equally like one another,
who all went in and out	/	at the same hours,
		with the same sound
		upon the same pavements,
		to do the same work,
and to whom every day	/	was the same as yesterday and tomorrow,
and every year	/	the counterpart of the last and the next.

This fairly long sentence consists of a series of balanced and parallel clauses and phrases and is characterised by strong rhythms that in places are almost like those of metrical verse ('at the same hours, with the same sound . . .'). It may be significant that, by the time he wrote *Hard Times*, Dickens had begun giving public readings of his work for charity; not long afterwards he was to begin doing so, on a large scale in England and America, for money. The style of the description of Coketown may be described as an *oral* style in that it demands to be read aloud, or at least to be 'heard' by the silent reader, in order to make its full impact: like the rhetoric of the political speaker or the preacher, it is more emphatic and insistent, and makes greater use of repetition and rhythm, than ordinary discourse.

Finally, we may note that, although the subject is a profoundly serious one and Dickens is genuinely indignant at the dehumanised and dehumanising ugliness and monotony of Coketown, the use of comic detail so characteristic of his work is even here in evidence – though comedy is now used as one of the devices of satire. The phrase 'pious warehouse' (line 32), for instance, is a comic paradox that contains a truth: the chapel is as ugly as a warehouse and has been built by people whose minds cannot rise above the strictly utilitarian. Though the 'bell in a bird-cage' (line 33) is offered as a concession to aesthetic qualities, its half-hearted absurdity is conveyed by the use of the word 'bird-cage': and the same applies to the architectural ornaments that are compared to 'florid wooden legs' (line 36). Such comic similes expose the empty pretensions of those who supposedly represent the finer official feelings of Coketown: and, again, external objects are seen as reflecting the inner spirit and motivations of those who have created Coketown.

6 CRITICAL RECEPTION

Contemporary reviewers were generally unenthusiastic about *Hard Times*: as a successor to *David Copperfield* and *Bleak House*, it was perhaps inevitably found disappointing, and the social and political issues on which it touches provoked some antagonism. The influential *Athenaeum* (12 August 1854) said that it was 'a good idea' but 'scarcely wrought out with Mr Dickens's usual felicity'. The good idea referred to was that man's deepest longings cannot be satisfied by an unrelieved diet of 'fact'; but this, the anonymous reviewer argued, is essentially 'a poetical conception', whereas Dickens had given it 'a prosaic framework' peopled with 'very repulsive and vulgar characters'. The reviewer developed his point by stating that 'the case of Fancy *versus* Fact is here stated in prose, but without the fairness which belongs to a prose argument'. He evidently felt that there was a disastrous disharmony between Dickens's 'message' and the kind of novel he had chosen to accommodate it: he had fallen between the two stools of a thorough-going poetic or allegorical treatment, in which some simplification of the issues and a stylised presentation would have been acceptable, and the realistic mode of the novel, in which the case for both sides ought to be more fully and scrupulously given. (For example, it might have been indicated that not all employers were as outrageously unjust and unsympathetic as Bounderby – and that a circus does not offer a practical model on which most people can base their lives.)

Even more unfavourable was the verdict of Richard Simpson in *The Rambler* for October 1854. Simpson found the novel 'a mere full melodrama, in which character is caricature, sentiment tinsel, and moral (if any) unsound'. Dickens, he insisted, was a great entertainer but a poor instructor; and was at his weakest when he attempted to deal with a serious public theme, for 'he has never shown any ability to pierce the depths of social life, to fathom the wells of social action'. The intellectual monthly *Westminster Review* (October 1854) also found the characterisation weak: Bounderby was 'a most outrageous character', the whole Gradgrind family were 'unpleasant', and the death of Mrs Gradgrind was gratuitous ('it does not in any way assist the plot').

In contrast to these harsh judgements, John Forster, a close friend of Dickens, defended the novel – indeed, his review in *The Examiner* (9 September 1984) reads very much like a careful rejoinder to the *Athenaeum* review referred to. Forster insists that *Hard Times* does not present an argument because that is not the business of a novel ('no thesis can be argued in a novel'): what it does is to attempt to influence people for the better by working upon their feelings. Moreover, says Forster, it is a mistake to suppose that Dickens is against facts, for *Household Words*, which is under his editorship and in which *Hard Times* first appeared, is 'a great magazine of facts'. What Dickens deplores and attacks in the novel is an exclusive diet of facts that leaves no room in life for the 'fancy'.

A few years after the appearance of the novel, unexpected and very high praise for it came from John Ruskin, the critic of art and society whose influence on Victorian ideas was considerable. Ruskin makes the familiar complaint that Dickens's characters are exaggerated ('Mr Bounderby is a dramatic monster, instead of a characteristic example of a worldly master; and Stephen Blackpool a dramatic perfection, instead of a characteristic example of an honest workman'); and he expressed the wish that Dickens had used 'severer and more accurate analysis' in dealing with 'a subject of high national importance'. But then he declares that the novel is 'in several respects the greatest he has written', and that, despite the exaggeration and the failure to state both sides of a question fairly and fully, Dickens's view of the questions raised in *Hard Times* is fundamentally sound:

> He is entirely right in the main drift and purpose in every book he has written; and all of them, but especially *Hard Times*, should be studied with close and earnest care by persons interested in social questions. They will find much that is partial, and, because partial, apparently unjust; but if they examine all the evidence on the other side, which Dickens seems to overlook, it will appear,

after all their trouble, that his view was the finally right one. grossly and sharply told.

Ruskin's essay was first published in *The Cornhill Magazine* in August 1860, and was later included in his popular book *Unto This Last* (1862).

Notwithstanding Ruskin's high praise, the reputation of the novel for the next ninety years or so was generally low. An American critic, Edwin Whipple, writing in *The Atlantic Monthly* (March 1877), described Ruskin's claim that it was the greatest of Dickens's books as 'ridiculous' (to be fair, Ruskin had said 'in several respects'), and argued that the intellectual basis of the novel is damagingly weak. George Gissing, writing in 1898, described it as a 'very poor book' and 'practically a forgotten book'; and as late as 1941 Humphry House called it 'the least read of all the novels'. Two exceptions to this view must be noted. In his *Charles Dickens* (1906), the popular essayist and critic G. K. Chesterton said that *Hard Times* 'strikes an almost unexpected note of severity', and defended Dickens against the charge of exaggeration:

> The characters are indeed exaggerated but they are bitterly and deliberately exaggerated; they are not exaggerated with the old unconscious high spirits of Nicholas Nickleby or Martin Chuzzlewit. Dickens exaggerated Bounderby because he really hates him. . . . *Hard Times* is not one of the greatest books of Dickens: but it is perhaps in a sense one of his greatest monuments. It stamps and records the reality of Dickens's emotion on a great many things that were then considered unphilosophical grumblings, but which since have swelled into the immense phenomena of the socialist philosophy.

A similar argument was advanced a few years later by George Bernard Shaw, in his introduction to a 1912 edition of *Hard Times*, in which he claims for the novel a greater relevance to the state of contemporary Britain than any of its predecessors:

> England is full of Bounderbys and . . . Gradgrinds, and we are all to a quite appalling extent in their power. We either fear them or else we are them, and resent being held up to odium by a novelist. . . . *Hard Times* was written to make you uncomfortable; and

it will perhaps interest you more, and certainly leave a deeper scar on you, than any two of its forerunners.

Shaw is not uncritical of the book: he notes the non-realistic nature of much of the dialogue (Louisa is 'a figure of poetic tragedy' who talks like 'an inspired prophetess', and Sissy in her interview with Harthouse uses 'the language of a Lord Chief Justice, not of the dunce of an elementary school'); and he finds the presentation of Slackbridge to be a failure ('a mere figment of the middle-class imagination'). But the fact that he considered the novel to be worthy of such serious and sustained attention, and his insistence, from the point of view of a committed socialist, on its relevance to social issues two generations after its publication, is a striking tribute during a period of general neglect.

That neglect came dramatically to an end when F. R. Leavis included an essay on *Hard Times* in his widely influential study of the novel, *The Great Tradition* (1948). Leavis claims for this widely neglected novel a status that recalls, and indeed goes beyond, the claim made by Ruskin: for Leavis it is 'of all Dickens's works . . . the one that has all the strength of his genius, together with a strength no other of them can show – that of a completely serious work of art'. Not many subsequent critics have been prepared fully to endorse this judgement; but it had the effect of stimulating attention to one of Dickens's most neglected works, and is perhaps largely responsible for the wide currency the novel now enjoys as a text for study.

Leavis regards *Hard Times* as a 'masterpiece' showing 'an astonishing and irresistible richness of life'. Although conceding that there are weaknesses in the presentation of the trade-union movement and of Stephen Blackpool, he finds in it 'a clear insight into the English social structure'; and he implicitly answers those earlier critics, such as Shaw, who found much of the characterisation and dialogue unconvincing by arguing that the novel 'affects us as belonging with formally poetic works'. This is a very important point, since, if accepted, it affects our entire approach to the novel. Leavis writes:

> . . . *Hard Times* is a poetic work. It suggests that the genius of the writer may fairly be described as that of a poetic dramatist, and that, in our preconceptions about 'the novel', we may miss, within the field of fictional prose, possibilities of concentration and

flexibility in the interpretation of life such as we associate with Shakespearean drama.

Hard Times belongs, that is to say, not to the mode of realism – the 'imitation of life' in which authenticity and plausibility are all-important – that is the mainstream of the English tradition of fiction, but to a more stylised and 'poetic' kind of art that is closer to *King Lear* than to *Vanity Fair* or *Middlemarch*. Interestingly enough, Leavis has revived the debate initiated in the very first critical verdict cited in this chapter, The *Athenaeum* review published very soon after *Hard Times* first appeared in volume form. Leavis's essay was reprinted, with an appendix responding to some of the challenges made to it, in *Dickens the Novelist* (1970) by F. R. and Q. D. Leavis.

Since 1948 *Hard Times* has received its fair share of attention from Dickens's critics, and there has been some useful research into the real-life background of the novel – one of the effects of which has been to show that in, for instance, his account of the teaching methods used in the schools for the poor, Dickens was not guilty of exaggeration. Two essays representing different points of view may be briefly mentioned. In 'The Rhetoric of *Hard Times*' in his *Language of Fiction* (1966), David Lodge finds both strengths and weaknesses in this 'polemical novel', and suggests that the weaknesses derive from a failure to devise stylistic means to serve his purposes ('Dickens's rhetoric is only partially adequate to the tasks he set himself'). In the introduction to his Penguin edition of the novel (1969), David Craig offers a Marxist reading and adduces much interesting material relating to the social, educational and industrial background. His conclusion is that

> if one tried to imagine the great industrial novel that never did get written, one might suggest that the masters cried out to be satirized, the mass of the people to be presented with clear-eyed realism. In so far as Dickens fails in the latter, his novel sags; in so far as he excels in the former, it succeeds, and thereby earns the currency which has made 'Coketown' the classic name for the early-industrial city.

As these two different verdicts show, recent assessments of the novel have found a middle course between the denigration and neglect of many of its earlier critics and the inflated claims made for it by Ruskin and Leavis. It is a work of great power and is unmistakably stamped with the signs of Dickens's genius during the period of his maturity; but it would be foolish to claim that it is flawless or that it possesses the range and variety of his longer and more ambitious depictions of society.

A notable French scholar, Sylvère Monod, has summed up the strange critical fortunes of *Hard Times* by saying that its 'critical history . . . is astonishing, and it is quite an education to contemplate it'. Although the examples cited in this chapter represent only a selection of the critical verdicts of the past 130 years, they may suggest the wide range of reactions it has provoked and some of the reasons for this diversity of response. Probably no other of Dickens's novels has been, at various times, so harshly attacked, so neglected and so highly praised. Many of the items referred to in this chapter are included in the volume on *Hard Times*, *Great Expectations* and *Our Mutual Friend* in the Casebook series (1979), edited by Norman Page.

REVISION QUESTIONS

1. On 13 July 1854, Dickens wrote to Thomas Carlyle (to whom *Hard Times* is dedicated): 'It contains what I do devoutly hope will shake some people in a terrible mistake of these days, when so presented.' What 'terrible mistake' is he thinking of, and how is the issue 'presented' in the novel?

2. What attitudes towards industrialism and the life of the factory-worker does Dickens express?

3. Some of the early critics of *Hard Times* complained that, though Dickens dealt with serious social questions, he did not fairly state the arguments on both sides of those questions. Does this seem to you to be a fair criticism of the novel?

4. Explain why Dickens chose to open the novel in a schoolroom. Your answer should show the importance in the novel of education in both the narrower and the broader senses of the word.

5. How does Dickens provide connections between the plot and sub-plot of *Hard Times*?

6. Discuss Dickens's methods of presenting and individualising his characters, with detailed reference to at least three characters.

7. It has been said that Gradgrind is the only example in all Dickens's novels of the intellectual or man of ideas. What ideas does he represent, and how does Dickens transform them into a dramatic narrative?

8. Show the importance of the following in *Hard Times*: (a) Sissy Jupe; (b) Bitzer; (c) Mrs Sparsit; (d) Slackbridge.

9. 'Although Gradgrind and Bounderby are in some respects similar, Dickens distinguishes carefully between them.' Examine this statement with close reference to the novel.

10. How far does Dickens present a cross-section of different social levels and indicate the differences between them?
11. What is the importance of the circus in *Hard Times*?
12. What part in *Hard Times* is played by (a) comedy, (b) pathos?

FURTHER READING

John Butt and Kathleen Tillotson, *Dickens at Work* (London: Methuen, 1957). (Includes a chapter on *Hard Times*.)

Philip Collins, *Dickens and Education* (London: Macmillan, 1963).

Humphry House, *The Dickens World* (London: Oxford University Press, 1941).

F. R. Leavis, *The Great Tradition* (London: Chatto & Windus, 1948).

Further references will be found in Chapter 6, above. Early criticisms of *Hard Times* are collected in *Dickens: The Critical Heritage*, ed. Philip Collins (London: Routledge & Kegan Paul, 1970). Selections of critical material will be found in the Norton Critical Edition of *Hard Times*, edited by George Ford and Sylvère Monod (New York: Norton, 1966), and in the Casebook referred to on p. 79 above. Angus Wilson's *The World of Charles Dickens* (London: Secker & Warburg, 1970) is a lively and well-illustrated account of Dickens and his times, and Norman Page's *A Dickens Companion* (London: Macmillan, 1984) is a guide to the whole of Dickens's work.

MACMILLAN STUDENTS' NOVELS

General Editor: JAMES GIBSON

The Macmillan Students' Novels are low-priced, new editions of major classics, aimed at the first examination candidate. Each volume contains:

* enough explanation and background material to make the novels accessible — and rewarding — to pupils with little or no previous knowledge of the author or the literary period;

* detailed notes elucidate matters of vocabulary, interpretation and historical background;

* eight pages of plates comprising facsimiles of manuscripts and early editions, portraits of the author and photographs of the geographical setting of the novels.

Also from Macmillan

CASEBOOK SERIES

The Macmillan *Casebook* series brings together the best of modern criticism with a selection of early reviews and comments. Each Casebook charts the development of opinion on a play, poem, or novel, or on a literary genre, from its first appearance to the present day.

GENERAL THEMES

COMEDY: DEVELOPMENTS IN CRITICISM
D. J. Palmer

DRAMA CRITICISM: DEVELOPMENTS SINCE IBSEN
A. J. Hinchliffe

THE ENGLISH NOVEL: DEVELOPMENTS IN CRITICISM SINCE HENRY JAMES
Stephen Hazell

THE LANGUAGE OF LITERATURE
N. Page

THE PASTORAL MODE
Bryan Loughrey

THE ROMANTIC IMAGINATION
J. S. Hill

TRAGEDY: DEVELOPMENTS IN CRITICISM
R. P. Draper

POETRY

WILLIAM BLAKE: SONGS OF INNOCENCE AND EXPERIENCE
Margaret Bottrall

BROWNING: MEN AND WOMEN AND OTHER POEMS
J. R. Watson

BYRON: CHILDE HAROLD'S PILGRIMAGE AND DON JUAN
John Jump

CHAUCER: THE CANTERBURY TALES
J. J. Anderson

COLERIDGE: THE ANCIENT MARINER AND OTHER POEMS
A. R. Jones and W. Tydeman

DONNE: SONGS AND SONETS
Julian Lovelock

T. S. ELIOT: FOUR QUARTETS
Bernard Bergonzi

T. S. ELIOT: PRUFROCK, GERONTION, ASH WEDNESDAY AND OTHER POEMS
B. C. Southam

T. S. ELIOT: THE WASTELAND
C. B. Cox and A. J. Hinchliffe

ELIZABETHAN POETRY: LYRICAL AND NARRATIVE
Gerald Hammond

THOMAS HARDY: POEMS
J. Gibson and T. Johnson

GERALD MANLEY HOPKINS: POEMS
Margaret Bottrall

KEATS: ODES
G. S. Fraser

KEATS: THE NARRATIVE POEMS
J. S. Hill

MARVELL: POEMS
Arthur Pollard

THE METAPHYSICAL POETS
Gerald Hammond

THACKERAY: VANITY FAIR
Arthur Pollard

TROLLOPE: THE BARSETSHIRE NOVELS
T. Bareham

VIRGINIA WOOLF: TO THE LIGHTHOUSE
Morris Beja

DRAMA

CONGREVE: COMEDIES
Patrick Lyons

T. S. ELIOT: PLAYS
Arnold P. Hinchliffe

JONSON: EVERY MAN IN HIS HUMOUR AND THE ALCHEMIST
R. V. Holdsworth

JONSON: VOLPONE
J. A. Barish

MARLOWE: DR FAUSTUS
John Jump

MARLOWE: TAMBURLAINE, EDWARD II AND THE JEW OF MALTA
John Russell Brown

MEDIEVAL ENGLISH DRAMA
Peter Happé

O'CASEY: JUNO AND THE PAYCOCK, THE PLOUGH AND THE STARS AND THE SHADOW OF A GUNMAN
R. Ayling

JOHN OSBORNE: LOOK BACK IN ANGER
John Russell Taylor

WEBSTER: THE WHITE DEVIL AND THE DUCHESS OF MALFI
R. V. Holdsworth

WILDE: COMEDIES
W. Tydeman

SHAKESPEARE

SHAKESPEARE: ANTONY AND CLEOPATRA
John Russell Brown

SHAKESPEARE: CORIOLANUS
B. A. Brockman

SHAKESPEARE: HAMLET
John Jump

SHAKESPEARE: HENRY IV PARTS I AND II
G. K. Hunter

SHAKESPEARE: HENRY V
Michael Quinn

SHAKESPEARE: JULIUS CAESAR
Peter Ure

SHAKESPEARE: KING LEAR
Frank Kermode

SHAKESPEARE: MACBETH
John Wain

SHAKESPEARE: MEASURE FOR MEASURE
G. K. Stead

SHAKESPEARE: THE MERCHANT OF VENICE
John Wilders

SHAKESPEARE: A MIDSUMMER NIGHT'S DREAM
A. W. Price

SHAKESPEARE: MUCH ADO ABOUT NOTHING AND AS YOU LIKE IT
John Russell Brown

SHAKESPEARE: OTHELLO
John Wain

SHAKESPEARE: RICHARD II
N. Brooke

SHAKESPEARE: THE SONNETS
Peter Jones

SHAKESPEARE: THE TEMPEST
D. J. Palmer

SHAKESPEARE: TROILUS AND CRESSIDA
Priscilla Martin

SHAKESPEARE: TWELFTH NIGHT
D. J. Palmer

SHAKESPEARE: THE WINTER'S TALE
Kenneth Muir

MILTON: PARADISE LOST
A. E. Dyson and Julian Lovelock

POETRY OF THE FIRST WORLD
WAR
Dominic Hibberd

ALEXANDER POPE: THE RAPE OF
THE LOCK
John Dixon Hunt

SHELLEY: SHORTER POEMS &
LYRICS
Patrick Swinden

SPENSER: THE FAERIE QUEEN
Peter Bayley

TENNYSON: IN MEMORIAM
John Dixon Hunt

THIRTIES POETS: 'THE AUDEN
GROUP'
Ronald Carter

WORDSWORTH: LYRICAL
BALLADS
A. R. Jones and W. Tydeman

WORDSWORTH: THE PRELUDE
W. J. Harvey and R. Gravil

W. B. YEATS: POEMS 1919–1935
E. Cullingford

W. B. YEATS: LAST POEMS
Jon Stallworthy

THE NOVEL AND PROSE

JANE AUSTEN: EMMA
David Lodge

JANE AUSTEN: NORTHANGER
ABBEY AND PERSUASION
B. C. Southam

JANE AUSTEN: SENSE AND
SENSIBILITY, PRIDE AND
PREJUDICE AND MANSFIELD
PARK
B. C. Southam

CHARLOTTE BRONTË: JANE EYRE
AND VILLETTE
Miriam Allott

EMILY BRONTË: WUTHERING
HEIGHTS
Miriam Allott

BUNYAN: THE PILGRIM'S
PROGRESS
R. Sharrock

CONRAD: HEART OF DARKNESS,
NOSTROMO AND UNDER
WESTERN EYES
C. B. Cox

CONRAD: THE SECRET AGENT
Ian Watt

CHARLES DICKENS: BLEAK
HOUSE
A. E. Dyson

CHARLES DICKENS: DOMBEY
AND SON AND LITTLE DORRITT
Alan Shelston

CHARLES DICKENS: HARD TIMES,
GREAT EXPECTATIONS AND OUR
MUTUAL FRIEND
N. Page

GEORGE ELIOT: MIDDLEMARCH
Patrick Swinden

GEORGE ELIOT: THE MILL ON
THE FLOSS AND SILAS MARNER
R. P. Draper

HENRY FIELDING: TOM JONES
Neil Compton

E. M. FORSTER: A PASSAGE TO
INDIA
Malcolm Bradbury

HARDY: THE TRAGIC NOVELS
R. P. Draper

HENRY JAMES: WASHINGTON
SQUARE AND THE PORTRAIT OF
A LADY
Alan Shelston

JAMES JOYCE: DUBLINERS AND A
PORTRAIT OF THE ARTIST AS A
YOUNG MAN
Morris Beja

D. H. LAWRENCE: THE RAINBOW
AND WOMEN IN LOVE
Colin Clarke

D. H. LAWRENCE: SONS AND
LOVERS
Gamini Salgado

SWIFT: GULLIVER'S TRAVELS
Richard Gravil

THE MACMILLAN SHAKESPEARE

General Editor: PETER HOLLINDALE
Advisory Editor: PHILIP BROCKBANK

The Macmillan Shakespeare features:
* clear and uncluttered texts with modernised punctuation and spelling wherever possible;
* full explanatory notes printed on the page facing the relevant text for ease of reference;
* stimulating introductions which concentrate on content, dramatic effect, character and imagery, rather than mere dates and sources.

Above all, The Macmillan Shakespeare treats each play as a work for the theatre which can also be enjoyed on the page.

MACMILLAN SHAKESPEARE VIDEO WORKSHOPS

DAVID WHITWORTH

Three unique book and video packages, each examining a particular aspect of Shakespeare's work; tragedy, comedy and the Roman plays. Designed for all students of Shakespeare, each package assumes no previous knowledge of the plays and can serve as a useful introduction to Shakespeare for 'O' and 'A' level candidates as well as for students at colleges and institutes of further, higher and adult education.

The material is based on the New Shakespeare Company Workshops at the Roundhouse, adapted and extended for television. By combining the resources of television and a small theatre company, this exploration of Shakespeare's plays offers insights into varied interpretations, presentation, styles of acting as well as useful background information.

While being no substitute for seeing the whole plays in performance, it is envisaged that these video cassettes will impart something of the original excitement of the theatrical experience, and serve as a welcome complement to textual analysis leading to an enriched and broader view of the plays.

Each package consists of:

* the Macmillan Shakespeare editions of the plays concerned;

* a video cassette available in VHS or Beta;

* a leaflet of teacher's notes.

THE TORTURED MIND
looks at the four tragedies Hamlet, Othello, Macbeth and King Lear.

THE COMIC SPIRIT ·
examines the comedies Much Ado About Nothing, Twelfth Night, A Midsummer Night's Dream, and As You Like It.

THE ROMAN PLAYS
Features Julius Caesar, Antony and Cleopatra
and Coriolanus